TEACHING AND ASSESSING IN CLINICAL NURSING PRACTICE

Edited by

Peter L. Bradshaw
Professor, School of Human and Health Sciences, University of Huddersfield

PRENTICE HALL

NEW YORK LONDON TORONTO SYDNEY TOKYO

First published 1989 by
Prentice Hall Europe
Campus 400, Maylands Avenue, Hemel Hempstead
Hertfordshire, HP2 7EZ
A division of
Simon & Schuster International Group

Printed and bound in Great Britain by
T.J. Press (Padstow) Ltd, Padstow, Cornwall.

British Library Cataloguing in Publication Data

Teaching and assessing in clinical nursing practice.
    1. Great Britain. Nurses. Professional
education. Curriculum. Planning
    I. Bradshaw, Peter L.
    610.73′07′1141

    ISBN 0–13–891425–7

    9 10 11   98 97 96

This book is dedicated to
the nurses of Dorset

CONTENTS

CONTRIBUTORS

Peter L. Bradshaw MA, B Nurs, RGN, RMN, NDN Cert, HV, RNT
  Professor, University of Huddersfield
Hilarv Brown, BA, RGN, DipN (Lond), RNT
  Nurse Tutor, Dorset School of Nursing
Janice Gosby MA, Cert Ed, Dip N (Lond), RGN, RCNT, RNT
  Senior Tutor, Dorset School of Nursing
Marion Moody BA, RGN, RM, Dip N (Lond), RCNT, RNT
  Tutor, Dorset School of Nursing
David J. Moore BA, RMN, RGN, Dip N (Lond), RNT
  Assistant Director of Nurse Education, Dorset School of Nursing
Gillian M. Skelton BA, RGN, RM, Dip N (Lond), Dip Ed (Lond), RNT
  Tutor, Dorset School of Nursing

PREFACE

This book is intended for any nurse who teaches others. It explores pertinent dilemmas in clinical nurse education and suggests many innovative solutions.

The book is the collective work of colleagues in the Dorset School of Nursing. The Dorset School has undertaken considerable pioneering work in nurse education by developing its registered general nurse (RGN) pilot scheme for mature students. This well established course pre-dates Project 2000 in its origins, but contains all the major features of nurse education's blueprint for the future. Students of the pilot scheme enjoy a common foundation programme with supernumerary status. Their academic work is taught in association with the Dorset Institute, a major academic institution which offers them an enhanced programme of educational study. The focus of their course however concerns the essentials of clinical practice. To produce expertise in students, it has been necessary properly to prepare experienced clinical practitioners to optimize their crucial contribution to this major matter. The authors of this book have had the privilege to work alongside their clinical colleagues during their period of development. This book reflects that experience and explores the issues and the challenges which commonly arose.

Peter L. Bradshaw

ACKNOWLEDGEMENTS

The authors are deeply indebted to Mrs Anne Powell, Mrs Clare Long and Mrs Lynne Carpenter for their painstaking work in preparing this manuscript.

CHAPTER ONE

MARKING TIME – THE STATE OF NURSE EDUCATION IN THE UNITED KINGDOM

INTRODUCTION – UNDERSTANDING THE SYSTEM

This chapter concerns the system of nurse education in the United Kingdom organized within the National Health Service (NHS) in which the majority who aspire to nursing are trained. In reality, student nurses spend their training in two separate institutions. Approaching one sixth of a basic pre-registration course is spent in formal study about nursing and related subjects within a school of nursing. The remainder is spent working in the NHS and thereby, gaining practical experience.

This system of nurse training is fraught with difficulties. The title 'student nurse' is fundamentally invalid because the student is first and foremost a worker and an employee. Students are required to deal with the contingencies of the NHS and are thus exposed haphazardly to a wide range of experiences for which they receive no prior preparation. The term apprenticeship is frequently applied to nurse education. This is an equally inept description, because student nurses are not attached to a particular named expert to learn their craft and indeed, they have to learn a great deal from other students who are only slightly more experienced. Furthermore, student nurses have little opportunity to apply the slim theoretical component of their course to practice because they are moved regularly from one work location to another to meet service demands.

All in all, student nurses cultivate two versions of nursing. One perspective is educationally oriented and represents an idealized view of nursing and is used to satisfy their tutors and pass examinations. A second and sometimes competing view concerns actual nursing work in the wards. This latter view enables the student nurse to produce appropriate behaviours and to fit in with colleagues whose major concern is the work generated by patients (Melia, 1984).

REFORMING THE SYSTEM – THE MAJOR REPORTS

The essential nature of the UK system of nurse education has remained unchanged for a century. Radical amendment has been avoided on several occasions by government, the profession or both in favour of cosmetic stopgap measures to keep the system working. The system continues to rely on role, ritual and tradition so that the educational needs of its students are in constant tension with the staffing imperatives of NHS wards and departments.

The key deficiencies of the system have been long recognized, becoming the focus of major reports over the last four decades. Repeated serious and damning evidence has to date been ignored or discarded. The Horder Committee constituted by the Royal College of Nursing (RCN) pleaded for the training of student nurses to be separated from their obligation to staff hospital wards (Horder, 1943). The Committee identified clearly the contradictions when student nurses are also the essential workforce. A supplement to the Horder Report made the novel suggestion that nurse training should be linked to the newly evolving post-war system of general education (RCN, 1945).

The Wood Committee set up by the Ministry of Health in the light of the Horder report recommended gross educational reforms. It argued positively that student nurses be made supernumerary to manpower requirements in practical placements. Apart from alleged benefits for students, Wood argued this measure would effect economies in two ways. Firstly, supernumerary status was seen as a means to shorten training time to two years. Secondly, it claimed wastage would be reduced by up to a third. Regrettably the central thrust of Wood's recommendations was lost. A strong streak of anti-intellectualism permeated the powerful lobby of hospital matrons at the time and hence political support for the report was lacking (White, 1980).

By the early 1950s the NHS was struggling to contain its costs and the expensiveness of the nursing workforce came under scrutiny. The Nuffield Report on the work of nurses in hospital wards was ostensibly a job evaluation of nursing work. Yet it did produce penetrating observations concerning the training of student nurses. It concluded, for instance, that the time devoted to the teaching of student nurses in the wards was negligible.

By the 1950s, nursing had reached a curious position for a professional practice field by having tutors who did not practise nursing and ward sisters, who, though expert practitioners in theory, could not teach. The problem of integrating theory with practice and establishing improved links between education and service was approached by the creation of a new type of post. The clinical teacher emerged during the mid 1950s as a means to bridge the gap between what was taught in the classroom and that practised at the patient's bedside.

An important new development began in 1956 at Glasgow Royal Infirmary in an attempt to overcome the well recognized limitations of the nurse education and training system. A scheme was devised to contend with the twin problems of providing a proper education for student nurses without disrupting service delivery to patients (Scott-Wright, 1961). The Glasgow project provided considerable departures from conventional approaches. Its salient features were as follows:

1. Supernumerary status for students.
2. A closer relationship between theory and practice.
3. Financial independence of the school of nursing from its parent hospital.
4. Students were supervised by their tutors when giving care.

Several results emerged. Attrition was much lower than on traditional courses and it was demonstrated students could be prepared successfully for their final examination in two years rather than three (Scottish Home and Health Department, 1963).

The success of the Glasgow experiment, experiences of nurse education in North America and the general inadequacy and continued dissatisfaction with the UK system, precipitated the appointment of the Platt Committee by the RCN in 1961. The committee had a wide remit and reported three years later (Platt, 1964). Its emphatic recommendations concerned a two year grant-assisted studentship whereby students were independent financially of their parent hospital. A third year of practice under controlled supervision was to follow. Once again, the report, despite being initiated by the RCN, failed to gain the support of the profession. It indicated that the function of the General Nursing Council (GNC) would have to change to accommodate its suggested reforms, which provoked further anti-intellectual objections – this time from GNC that the needs of the patient must take precedence over the educational needs of students, and that the emphasis on student status would deter girls whose only wish was to nurse (GNC, 1965).

Platt was shelved and the student-led labour system remained undisturbed. A series of experiments continued in the form of two-year preparation with a final year to consolidate practical skills, the so-called 2+1 schemes. Interestingly all such innovations during the 1960s and 1970s recruited students much above average ability as measured by standardized intelligence tests. In retrospect it is peculiar how remedies to the problems of nurse education were sought through schemes which were not easily generalizable to conventional student populations of lower academic ability.

The late 1960s saw nursing's professional energies channelled into managerial reforms. The education system remained static save for a new syllabus of general nursing in 1969 which acted as a smokescreen to the real difficulties for some years. The debate between those wishing to improve the educational experience afforded students and those who required students to maintain the nursing service continued. Undercurrents were such as to lead the government to commission an official enquiry, the Committee on Nursing in 1970. The Committee, under the chairmanship of Professor Asa Briggs published its conclusions in 1972 (Briggs, 1972). The structural changes proposed by Briggs were far reaching. These envisaged an eighteen-month course leading to a certificate to practise, and a further eighteen months leading to registration. Briggs related training to the needs of the population emphasizing modular programmes to relate theory to practice, and stressing the importance of continuing education and research. In other educational respects such as supernumerary status, the report was less decisive.

Briggs did become, however, the forerunner for educational reform by preparing the way for the Nurses, Midwives and Health Visitors Act 1979. This legislation enabled the founding of a new unified statutory body, the United Kingdom Central Council for Nurses, Midwives and Health Visitors (UKCC). Despite the many years since the Briggs Report and the internecine warfare within the profession which has hindered progress, the possibility of reform looks more likely than before. UKCC was charged by statute to establish and improve standards of training. After wide consultation within the profession its conclusions on this emerged in the Project 2000 Report (UKCC, 1986). Between 1979 and 1986 impatience at the UKCC delay in producing concrete proposals led to an RCN Commission on Nurse Education (1985) and an English National Board (ENB) Consultation paper (ENB, 1985). Both of these exerted considerable influence on the Project 2000 findings and UKCC's recommendations to government in 1987.

The RCN Commissioners recommended the translation of current NHS schools of nursing and their staff into the mainstream of higher education. A new three-year preparation for nursing was proposed resulting in the award of a Diploma validated by the Council for National Academic Awards. The Commission contended that its proposals would make nursing more attractive in the labour market, with appeal to better educated recruits with a consequent reduction in wastage rates and a greatly improved calibre of practitioner. It claimed its recommendations would enable statutory bodies, DHSS and health authorities to relate training places more closely to manpower requirements. The Commission spoke of preserving at every stage, an engagement in practice to generate intelligent proficiency. It saw this being achieved through controlled education experiences in protected learning areas. It envisaged many other innovations to emphasize studentship rather than worker status, such as courses based on the pattern of a traditional academic year, with some extensions to fulfil necessary clinical placements. Hard on the heels of the RCN report came the ENB consultation paper (ENB, 1985). It advocated supernumerary student status for two out of three years. It anticipated moves from theory-centred teaching at the beginning of a course to an application-centred approach with measurable service giving at the end. Like the RCN Commissioners, ENB proposed links with the public education sector.

Project 2000 reached almost identical conclusions to the RCN Commissioners and the ENB Consultation paper, advocating supernumerary status, common foundation programmes and a rationalization of qualifications. The Project's solutions were, however, much less emphatic than those of the RCN Commissioners. While the Project argued for earmarked funds for nurse education, it intended to leave a great deal of administrative detail to the whim of the four National Boards.

The main thrust of all these reports in the last forty years is the desire to improve the quality of a student nurse's learning experience by providing a system based on sound educational principles. A shift in professional opinion has also occurred, so there is now broad dissatisfaction with the existing system. This shift is substantiated by scholarly research which has investigated the process of nurse education in great detail.

RESEARCH INTO THE PROCESS OF NURSE EDUCATION

The literature of the recent past isolates three major themes needing to be addressed in order for the processes of nurse education to be reformed.

1. The theory/practice dilemma

Some research has indicated that the disparities between theoretical aspects of nursing courses and practices in the wards produce frustration and discontent in students, leading to excessive absenteeism and withdrawal from training. MacGuire (1969) and Dalton (1969) studied students who had decided to leave training prematurely. Both revealed significant evidence that theoretical teachings are frequently inconsistent with ward practices. Similar discrepancies were discovered by Hunt (1971) concerning the specific instance of the carrying out of aseptic dressing procedures. Theoretical propositions about asepsis were ignored rendering some procedures potentially harmful to patients.

Birch (1972) identified stress and conflict originating from the differential practices of classroom and ward as an influential determinant of student attrition. This research suggested that the conflict between the teaching of the school of nursing and practices in the wards was being officially ignored. The work went on to suggest all teaching of nursing care be conducted in the wards rather than the school of nursing.

Jones (1975) identified variation between the teaching and practice of feeding techniques for patients who were unconscious. Deficient practices resulted in some patients receiving feeds inadequate in calories and furthermore, procedures for administering feeds were found to be dangerous to patients.

Alexander (1983) studied the integration of theory with practice using an experiment to compare a college-based programme with one which was ward-based. Evidence was produced advocating a ward-based approach, with more active involvement of tutors and students to produce positive links between what is taught and what is practised.

Theory in professional practice fields sets out to enquire and explain, and does not necessarily provide detailed prescriptions for practical action. Fond as nurse educators are of the notion of a knowledge base for nursing, there are many dimensions of current practice lacking a scientific explanation. These factors place inexperienced student nurses at a considerable disadvantage within the present system. Presently students frequently have to respond to the needs of individual patients by instinctive judgement. The present system lacks systematic attempts to show that the skilled practitioner is not programmed to respond to a predefined problem in a ritualistic and stereotyped way, but utilizes creative intellect to seek solutions to each problem.

2. Disparate expectations of the school of nursing and hospital service managers

The discrepancies between the ideals espoused by the school of nursing and the realities of the practice setting have been addressed by Bendall (1973). This work established that the activities nurses describe in their answers to examination questions in the school of nursing do not predict reliably what they will do in practice in the wards. These findings were made in programmes where theory was taught concurrently with relevant clinical practice. Such evidence indicates standards of practice in the wards to be unsatisfactory, or conversely, formal teaching may be unrealistic and unrelated to the changing nature of the ward environment.

Student nurses' perceptions of nurse education and nursing service have been investigated. Dodd (1974) found students valued the ward work as the reality of their working lives to the extent that the school of nursing and nurse teachers seemed almost irrelevant.

Harrison et al. (1977) reported on the integration of nursing theory with practice in modular schemes, and identified the different assumptions of service staff. But the report indicated ways the two can agree educational aims, and the central value of the ward sister to the educational process was highlighted.

Altschul (1978) was critical of nurse teachers because of their absence from the ward and inability to obtain feedback from their teaching. Altschul concluded that nurse teachers were becoming irrelevant to patient care.

Gott (1983) showed how nurse teachers failed to prepare student nurses for their job in the wards. This work is critical of the expectations placed upon student nurses by their school of nursing. It complains also about a system which allows the teaching of nursing by teachers who do not practice, suggesting that some teach unrealistic care because they are out of date.

3. The student as a worker

Several writers have investigated teaching and learning in the wards. Fretwell (1982) isolated necessary criteria for student learning to occur in their clinical placements.

This work reported traditional nursing hierarchies and routine practices to inhibit teaching and learning. By extension, an ideal learning environment may also inhibit the conduct of ward work. The research confirmed a relationship between workload and the occurrence of teaching and learning activities. Attitudes were also influential as learning took place more readily where students were regarded as learners rather than workers.

Further work concentrating on the ward sister as a crucial resource-person for teaching and learning was conducted by Ogier (1982). Attention focused on the leadership styles of sisters and the nature of their verbal interactions with student nurses. Sisters who perceived their students as learners rather than workers were reported by students as most helpful. Conflicts between the students' twin learner and worker roles were revealed with most students feeling more like workers for most of their training.

The ward learning climate was investigated by Orton (1981) using approaches from organizational psychology. The ward sister was established as central to the success of clinical placements. Orton added further evidence to the learner/worker divergence, discovering wards where students were seen purely as a source of labour.

The addition of these scholarly research findings to a series of learned reports all serves to reduce further confidence in a system of training wherein all reasonable educational considerations are frequently excluded. Project 2000 identifies a blueprint for the transformation of nurse education. What transformation potential, therefore, do its recommendations contain?

TOWARDS THE FUTURE

Despite the major constraints within the current system of nurse education, courses have become more educationally oriented. Student entrants are of good quality and teaching staff have a distinct willingness to study for degrees.

Project 2000 lays the foundation to permit nursing courses proper recognition, because at present, the qualification Registered Nurse is devoid of academic standing. There are several reasons for this. Schools of Nursing are isolated from the mainstream of education. Their service-dominated curricula and chaotic funding arrangements defy the rational development of student centred programmes of education expected of academically validated courses in the higher education sector.

The process to which students are exposed identified by the research literature compounds the poor image of nursing. Nursing is a professional practice field underpinned by a range of scientific disciplines. Yet the students' opportunity to study these essential bases to the understanding of clinical practice is negligible. Student nurses in England devote approximately nine weeks each year to their study of theory. This is less than the time for off-the-job training afforded to Youth Training Scheme participants, some of whom ironically, will become the nursing support workers of the future.

Some would argue the educational benefits and advantages of service-led, experiential training. The effects of clinical experience have been investigated extensively. The plethora of data to emerge establishes repeatedly that student nurses work mostly without adequate supervision or guidance. Their clinical experience contains a large element of time serving, that lacks any systematic attempt at the teaching of clinical competence.

The level of intellectual activity required of nursing students is regarded by observers outside the profession to be lacking in sufficient rigour to merit academic recognition and a proper academic award. Students enter training with good passes at GCE Ordinary Level. In three years the present system fails to take them to the academic equivalent of GCE Advanced Level, which marks the first rung of the academic ladder.

Project 2000 recommended joint professional and academic validation be pursued at the outset of educational change, in order that nursing qualifications gain standing. (Project 2000, recommendation 22 p. 73). This requires a central plan to move resources and NHS Schools of Nursing into the mainstream of higher education. The major validating body for academic qualifications, the Council for National Academic Awards (CNAA), could hardly countenance the approval of courses conducted solely in English Schools of Nursing at present.

Many schools of nursing lack the capacity to deliver the main recommendations of Project 2000. They lack 'critical mass'; that amalgam of people and resources necessary for a climate where advanced, academic/vocationally-related work may proceed, be nurtured and be sustained.

Project 2000 intimated a set of loose alliances between Schools of Nursing and higher education. A series of *ad hoc* arrangements could result in a system as second rate as the one that exists, and some Schools of Nursing could well fall prey to entrepreneurial college principals. With proper and systematic central planning, Schools of Nursing need not feel threatened and need not become lesser partners. Almost all will be strengthened and will thrive from stronger association with a wider academic community.

The association between higher education and Schools of Nursing has profound implications for the quality and delivery of nursing courses. It offers new opportunities to strengthen the teaching of nursing. It provides new academic credibility and backbone. Students of nursing are entitled to be taught the sciences underlying their practice by individuals who are experts in the respective disciplines. Higher education possesses this expertise. Furthermore, the involvement of academic colleagues who are not nurses frees nurse tutors to teach nursing. Nurse tutors in the NHS presently teach for up to forty-six weeks of each year, and are in direct contact with students for up to twenty-five hours each week. Their teaching covers a vast range of subjects which tend by necessity to be handled at a descriptive level whereby knowledge is not perceived as problematic.

There is no expectation that these colleagues will pursue research. This undermines and mocks the whole concept that nursing should become a research-based profession. In contrast, higher education teachers teach for thirty-six weeks each year and are in contact with their students for fifteen hours each week. They teach specialized subjects from the basis of research wherein knowledge is constantly seen as a problem. It is an expectation that higher education colleagues will pursue research or other forms of independent scholarship.

The academic standard of nursing can be directly related to standards of practice. The liberation of tutors to become teachers of nursing on courses linked to a credible academic award, will give students the form of education to which they are entitled. The mission of those who teach nursing in the future, therefore, is to instil disciplines of systematic enquiry and critical reflection which provide the developing practitioner with the basic attributes of good practice.

The elevation of nurse education may cause alarm among more conservative elements of the profession. The traditional adage that nursing requires people solely with common sense is an outdated argument needing to be dispelled. The medical scientific basis of nursing work is more complex and patients are better informed. Recruits are of a better quality than in former years and indeed many seek a more challenging course of study. Yet for many practitioners these future possibilities produce erroneous myths.

The achievement of supernumerary status and a new relationship with higher education does not mean students of nursing will spend all their time in a classroom or laboratory. Clinical experience will continue to be the salient feature of courses. New ENB Pilot Schemes (ENB, 1984) are showing how Schools of Nursing and higher education can work together to produce clinically-related courses of a high standard. In each of these, nurse tutors act as a fulcrum between academic knowledge and patient care by introducing students to the interactions between theory and practice.

Improved status for nursing courses and the award of recognized academically valid qualifications does not mean all nurses will become graduates. Individual centres will have freedom to determine at what level their courses should be pitched. Of the pilot schemes, two are geared towards a terminal award at the diploma level, one aims at the certificate level. Such innovations are not intentionally elitist. Students choosing to nurse surely deserve preparation in an unstressful student-centred environment that gives a qualification possessing some meaning.

CONCLUSION

The present system of nurse education has had its day. The system has to be seen within the context of the NHS. This complex service rendering organization has had no time for education for its nurses in the past. General managers, despite their commitment to quality and standards of service are charged to extract the maximum possible labour from the cheapest workforce. The system passing as nurse education is purely a cheap means to a manpower end. The time has come for nurse education to be placed on a sound academic basis, as there are now no defensible reasons why nurses need not be well educated for their role. It is appropriate that nurses assume their rightful role within traditional scholarly communities in higher education. As Clay reminds us after all: 'Vets are trained in higher education!' (Clay, 1987).

REFERENCES

Alexander, M. F. (1983). *Learning to Nurse: Integrating Theory and Practice*. London: Churchill-Livingstone.

Altschul, A. (1978). *A Measure of Education*. Paper given at the annual conference of the Royal College of Nursing, Association of Nurse Education, London.

Bendall, E. D. R. (1973). 'The relationship between recall and application of learning in trainee nurses'. PhD thesis, University of London.

Birch, J. A. (1972). 'An investigation into the cause and wastage during nurse training'. MEd. thesis, University of Newcastle-on-Tyne.

Briggs, A. (Chairman), (1972). Report of the Committee on Nursing. London: HMSO.

Clay, T. (1987). *Nurses, Power and Politics*. London: Heinemann.

Dalton, B. M. (1969). 'Withdrawal from training of RNMS student nurses', *Nursing Times*, Occasional Paper 2, 65, 3.

Dodd, A. (1974). 'Towards an understanding of nursing'. PhD thesis, University of London.

English National Board. Circular to pilot schemes.

English National Board (1985). Professional Education/Training Courses: Consultation Paper. London: ENB.

Fretwell, J. E. (1982). *Ward Teaching and Learning*. London: Royal College of Nursing.

General Nursing Council, (1965) 'Comments on the Platt Report', *Nursing Times*, 1 October 1965.

Gott, M. (1983). 'Preparation of the student for learning in the clinical setting' in *Research into Nurse Education*, Bryn Davis (ed.), Chapter 6, pages 106–28, Beckenham: Croom Helm.

Harrison, J. *et al.* (1977). 'Integrating theory and practice in modular schemes for basic nurse education', *Journal of Advanced Nursing*, 2, 5, 503–19.

Horder (Chairman) (1943). Nursing Reconstruction Committee, Report. London: Royal College of Nursing.

Hunt, J. M. (1971). *The Teaching and Practice of Basic Nursing Procedures in Three Hospitals*. MPhil thesis, University of Surrey.

Jones, D. (1975). *Food for Thought*. London: Royal College of Nursing.

MacGuire, J. (1969). *Threshold to Nursing*. Occasional Papers on Social Administration, No. 30. London: Bell.

Melia, K. (1984). 'Student nurses' construction of occupational socialisation', *Sociology of Health and Fitness* 6, 132–50.

Nuffield Provincial Hospitals Trust (1953). *Work of Nurses in Hospital Wards*, Report of a Job Analysis. London: Nuffield.

Ogier, M. E. (1982). *An Ideal Sister: A study of Leadership Styles and Verbal Interactions of Ward Sisters with Nurse Learners in General Hospitals*. London: Royal College of Nursing.

Orton, H. (1981). 'Ward learning climate and student response' in *Research into Nurse Education*, Bryn Davis (ed.), Chapter 5, pages 90–150. Beckenham: Croom Helm.

Platt, H. (Chairman) (1964). *A Reform of Nurse Education*, Report. London: Royal College of Nursing.

Royal College of Nursing (1945). *Nursing Reconstruction Committee Supplements to the Report on Education and Training*. London: Royal College of Nursing.

Royal College of Nursing (1985). *The Education of Nurses: A New Dispensation*. London: Royal College of Nursing.

Scottish Home & Health Department (1963). *Experimental Nursing Training at Glasgow Royal Infirmary*. Edinburgh: HMSO.

Scott-Wright, M. (1961). 'A study of the performance of student nurses in relation to a new method of training with special reference to the evaluation of an experimental course of basic nurse education being conducted in Scotland'. PhD thesis, University of Edinburgh.

United Kingdom Central Council (1986). *Project 2000: A New Preparation for Practice.* London: UKCC.

United Kingdom Central Council (1986). *Project 2000: A New Preparation for Practice*, Recommendation 22 page 73. London: UKCC.

White, R. (1980). *Post-war Reconstruction of Nursing.* RCN Research Society Conferences 1980.

Wood, R. (Chairman) (1945). *Working Party on the Recruitment and Training of Nurses.* Report of the Interdepartmental Working Party, Ministry of Health, London.

CHAPTER TWO

WHAT IS THIS THING CALLED NURSING? CONCEPTS, MODELS AND THEORIES FOR PRACTICE

INTRODUCTION

To understand and justify nursing may initially seem a daunting, confusing, even frustrating task. This is partly due to the language used. Nursing lacks its own technical language and so uses everyday words and manipulates their meanings to describe its purpose. Nursing is not a profession in the precise sense. In order to emerge as a fully fledged profession, nursing must continue to develop and clarify both its activities and their meanings. To understand and use nursing theory it is useful first to consider its basic terminology.

The language of nursing

The terms concept, model and theory are fundamental to the understanding of nursing. Used in their technical sense, these terms provide a genuine means to a more knowledgeable practice.

Concept

A concept is multifaceted. It is used to describe visible concrete objects such as a book. In addition it may define abstract notions and ideas which are fundamental to human life. Each concept describes a group of ideas or a class of objects.

A concept should display three formal qualities. Firstly a good concept is precise and can be expressed unambiguously. Secondly it should be possible to distinguish clearly when it does and does not apply. Thirdly it is useful in building a broader picture, a theory of some aspect of nursing practice. Using these standards nursing concepts do not rate highly. They are often vague, difficult to apply consistently and do not easily fit together into a coherent general pattern.

The concepts used in discussing nursing theory are mainly abstract. They consist of systematically ordered thoughts derived from our perceptions of life and experience. This presents an immediate problem because all nurses are different, so individual nurses are likely to describe nursing differently. Some examples of concepts which nurses commonly use are health, disease, society and the individual. Each of these words may evoke a different image in the mind of individual nurses. The difference in understanding stems from a wide variety of factors, including the society in which the nurse grew up, her present roles, both professional and personal, her level of awareness and education.

Although concepts are useful in so far as they help define the content of nursing work, unless some organization or explicit description of their relationships is made, their usefulness to nursing practice is limited. The relationship of concepts to a theory has already been acknowledged; the relationship to a model is suggested in Fig. 2.1.

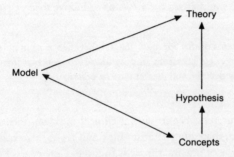

Fig. 2.1 Relationship between concepts, model and theory (1)

Theory
The term theory is derived from the Greek word *theoria*, meaning vision, and involves the uncovering of truth. Theories begin as single or groups of ideas, in nursing these usually concern some everyday practical activity. Take for example, the ways nurses influence the quality of care. The search considers the current situation, for instance the important consideration of skin care. The results of the search suggest a tentative reason for maintaining or improving the integrity of the skin, as the result of clinical practice. This is called a hypothesis.

A nursing theory, like theories in other disciplines, is based on rigorous experimentation. Experiments are designed in order that the factors believed to contribute to the ideal situation are isolated and their relative merits assessed. For instance in the case of skin care the diet, mobility and continence of a large number of people is assessed and the relationship between those factors reasonably established. The theory which emerges can therefore be both explanatory and to some extent predictive in nature. Most nurses are capable of expressing why they believe in certain actions. These beliefs often stem from tradition rather than research. But the body of knowledge on which true professions are based is derived from theory which is research-based. Some attempts to establish the unique nursing body of knowledge in this way have been undertaken using the two approaches to theoretical thinking which exist, namely deductive and inductive.

Deductive theory

Firstly, the deductive type of theory, which begins with some general concepts and proceeds to specific deductions. For example, 'The earth is flat' leads to the assumption that 'people who sail off the edge will fall off'. This approach in relation to nursing theory may involve selecting relevant concepts from other disciplines, for example psychology and physiology and relating them to specific nursing activities. Examples of deductive nursing theory are found in *Information – A Prescription Against Pain* (Hayward, 1975) and *A Prescription for Recovery* (Boore, 1978). In the latter physiological measurements were used to assess post-operative levels of stress.

Murphy (1971) summarizes the views of deductive theoreticians by suggesting that:

> in essence proponents of this approach suggest that theorizing in nursing is the result of modification, reconceptualisation and synthesis of concepts from other fields of knowledge as they describe and predict nursing practice.

Inductive theory

In this instance the nurse begins with a clinical problem, identifies the relevant concepts, describes their inter-relationships and from this evolves a theory. An example of this type of nursing theory is found in *Care of the Long Term Sick in the Community* (Kratz, 1978) in which Kratz allowed her data to generate a theory.

In nursing the body of knowledge acquired through the process leading to a theory is gradually increasing. A direct result of this is not only that nursing is beginning to meet one of the criteria considered essential for a profession, but also that when used by practitioners it can guide and improve their clinical practice. One of the difficulties in describing nursing theory concerns its relationship to behavioural, biological and social sciences. Much of what is currently known about nursing encompasses these disciplines and has not been validated in relation to nursing work. Another difficulty is that the theories evolved to date do not form the basis of future predictions. Attempts to do this will involve defining the concepts more sharply and devising more reliable methods of research, so that both the theory and the overall body of knowledge are more clear.

Like all theories, nursing theories leave many unanswered questions and it is these which become the theories for future generations of nurses to explore. Popper, in *Conjectures and Refutations* (1972), describes the need to verify theories, to expose them to the test. This then becomes part of the infinite process of the refutation of one theory as the result of both new information and argument, and the evolution of another.

Nursing theories then, like species evolve over generations. Their ability to be productive depends on their adaptability and appropriateness at a point in time in a particular environment.

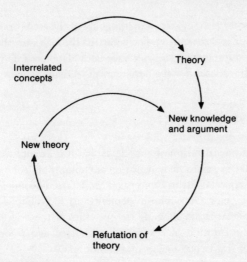

Fig. 2.2 The evolution of theories

Levels of theory
Not only can theories be described in terms of approach: deductive and inductive, but also in a hierarchy of four levels which reflect the purpose of the theory. Dickoff and James (1968) describe the levels as:

- factor-isolating theories
- factor-relating theories (situation depicting theories)
- situation-relating theories (predictive theories)
- situation-producing theories (prescriptive theories)

Each of these levels builds on those beneath it in the hierarchy. The lowest level – factor-isolating theory – is therefore most important and involves naming the factors – for example, devising a taxonomy of flowers.

The second level describes relationships between two factors, such as fluids and hydration, but only indicates that there is a relationship of sorts between them.

The third level, however, predicts that a number of factors such as physiological and mental conditions, activity and degree of continence are all causes and if assessed will predict the extent to which a person is at risk, for example, of developing pressure sores, as predicted in the Norton Scale.

The highest level is prescriptive; i.e. not only if A happens does B occur but also A is the cause of B and certain factors will facilitate A's causation of B. It is at this level that most nursing actions should occur and at which through using the nursing process they can occur. The characteristics of prescriptive theories include identification of a problem or need which will be resolved when a goal is achieved. This stage not only involves the need to survey a range of alternatives leading to the goal but to decide on which one to choose ultimately. A prescriptive theory also suggests something about the activities by which the goal may be achieved and that the choice is carried through into the implementation phase. Situation–producing theories have been elaborated by McFarlane (1980) and form the framework for the development of many models in nursing.

MODELS OF NURSING

A relatively simple definition of a model is that it is a simplified restructuring of reality undertaken to assist demonstration or exploration. A model is described by Hazzard and Kergin (1971) in *Conceptual Models for Nursing Practice* (Riehl and Roy, 1980) as being 'A symbolic depiction in logical terms of an idealized relatively simple situation showing the structure of the original system'. It is a conceptual representation of reality; an abstracted and reconstructed form of reality. It is not reality but a generalization of reality.

In everyday terms we are aware of different levels of models, for instance, models as scale replicas like the model of a new hospital on display; and of diagrams in a text book. Both these examples give an idea of the general purpose of models – to simplify a complex situation and to clarify components (factors) and their relationships as well as exploring the factors themselves. However, nursing models represent a higher level of model, in that they are conceptual frameworks, but like the models described above they simplify a complex situation, and help to identify and clarify the component parts and their interrelationships. They also enable the nurse to focus attention on the major aspects of the framework as well as making it possible for her to see it as a whole in concrete terms; because it is written down and involves for example, diagrams which are more easily assimilated. Perhaps the most creative aspect of a nursing model is that by using it as a framework it encourages colleagues to take a certain amount of licence with it and to experiment – what will happen if A takes place?

One of the difficulties that nurses experience is in deciding where models lie in relation to a concept—hypothesis—theory scheme. Numerous social scientists see

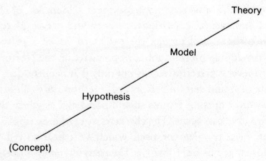

Fig. 2.3 Relationship between concepts, model and theory (2)

the use of models as an activity outside the hypothesis-theory hierarchy. Some see them as alternatives to theories, others view them in a hierarchy such as that depicted in Fig. 2.3.

Figure 2.1 is yet another alternative, in that it recognizes the link between each but acknowledges that models may not be part of the hierarchy, and yet they may contribute to the formation of a hypothesis.

TYPES OF MODEL

Nursing models began with Florence Nightingale who wrote her ideas in *Notes on Nursing* (1860) in an attempt to establish the concepts she believed to be important in a formal preparation to care for the sick during the second half of the nineteenth century. Since that time the concept of a model has evolved and diversified. It is worth considering why this should have occurred. Riehl and Roy suggest that conceptual models of nursing have developed over time as clarity, in so far as their essential elements are concerned, has improved specifically in relation to the goal of nursing, the concept of the patient and the mode of nursing intervention. Clarifying these concepts has naturally influenced nurse education, research and practice.

Even a cursory glance at a book about nursing theories and models will identify three types of models – systems, developmental and interactionist. These terms are used as a means of classifying the assumptions and values on which the model is based.

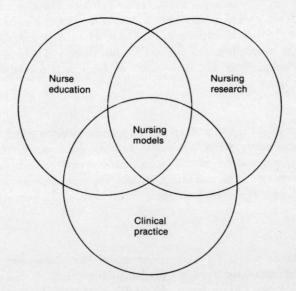

Fig. 2.4 Spheres of influence of nursing models

Systems models of nursing

Systems models of nursing view man as a collection of interrelated, biological, psychological and social systems. The systems model is based on the assumption that the interrelated parts are connected to each other in an organized way with a tendency to behave as a whole, in a state of equilibrium. Changes therefore within the system produce stress and tension. The notion of such a system suggests that it has limits – boundaries. The energy is primarily within these boundaries, although the system is obviously influenced by factors outside it, i.e. in the environment. The boundaries are moveable. Systems theorists argue that nursing is likely to be required when imbalance exists within or between the functions for which these systems are responsible and also to facilitate patient adaptation. Two of the most well known biological systems models are Roper *et al.* (1985) and Henderson (1972).

Roper

Roper's model is perhaps the most commonly used model in this country. The model adopts a holistic approach to the understanding of human needs but describes the activities which follow from these needs within a different framework from that used by, for example, Orem. Roper identifies four major components in the model, each of which can influence how care is delivered.

The model comprises twelve activities of living (including dying) which may be influenced by any of five factors, physiological, psychological, sociocultural, environmental and politicoeconomic. The activities are also influenced by age – so a lifespan continuum forms the third component, while the last is concerned with the patients' dependency in relation to each activity. This continuum ranges from total dependence to independence and is the fourth factor to be considered when deciding individualized nursing care. The problems are described in terms of changes in the environment and personal routine, changes in habit, in mode, in dependence/independence and as the result of discomforts associated with the activities of living.

Neuman

The Neuman model is also an example of a systems model in which the goal is system stability before, during or as a result of stress. The stress may be unique to the person/system or as the result of interaction between boundaries, i.e. between two people/systems, or because of, for instance, the social situation in which the person is living. The desired outcome is to increase the person's/system's resistance to stress.

Roy

Roy's adaptation model is a third systems model. Here the systems are clearly identified and interrelated biological, psychological and social systems within any one individual, hence Roy refers to the model as a bio-psycho-social model of nursing. The three systems exist in a state of constant interaction with the environment with which they are trying to maintain an equilibrium, and like Neumann's model are concerned with adapting to a changed situation. Roy identifies three types of stimulus that can affect the biopsychosocial being which may lead to failure to adapt because the person's coping mechanism fails. The problems which ensue from this failure to adapt may be viewed as points on a continuum from physiological problems, for example fever to hypothermia to such things as emotional experiences. For example, as a result of the focal stimulus such as behaviour of the nurse herself, the patient's behaviour includes occasional incontinence, a feeling of powerlessness and of rejection. These three problems reflect a failure to establish some sort of balance in the patient to the behaviour of a nurse. The patient in this model is the adapted system, the nurse's role is to support and promote adaptation.

Orem

Orem's model is considered by some to be a systems model although Fawcett (1984) claims that it is possible to find developmental emphasis in Orem's model. The model is defined as a self-care systems model since it focuses on nursing systems. There are three levels of assistance or approach that the nurse adopts to assist the patient with particular self-care deficits. These are described as wholly compensatory, partially compensatory and educative-supportive.

Developmental models of nursing

One of the earliest American theorists to evolve a model was Hildegard Peplau (1952). The values and assumptions in her model are of personal development both in the nurse and the patient as the result of their relationship and interactions. The goal of nursing she describes as being towards self actualisation which she states is not obtainable as long as unmet needs impede the onward and upward movement of the personality. According to the developmental perspective, nursing intervention is required when ill health or disease threatens the developmental process. At such times the role of the nurse will be in restoring the normal pattern of development and maturation, not only in a physical sense but psychologically and socially as well.

Interactionist models of nursing

Aggleton and Chalmers (1987) describe interactionist models of nursing as being different from both systems and developmental models, since their emphasis is on man's capacity to communicate in ways that are meaningful. They suggest that 'by focusing on people's capacity to interact with one another via symbols such as words, images and signs many (but not all) examples of this type of nursing model work with insights derived from a group of social scientists called symbolic interactionists, for example Cooley (1909)'. One of the better known

Interactionist nursing models is the Riehl Symbolic Interaction Model, which emphasizes man's psychological needs, and in particular his need to make sense of his immediate experiences psychologically. It involves the nurse trying to see and understand events through the patient's eyes, to understand the range of role behaviour options available to the patient. This model might be used for instance when the nurse considers the patient is displaying inappropriate behaviours in the hope that the patient will modify his behaviour as he begins to give appropriate symbolic meaning to the illness and the role which he has adapted to cope with this.

Why nursing models reflect on a number of concepts is worth a brief consideration. Little attempt has been made to place any of the models mentioned in chronological order. Undoubtedly date, the professional background of the author as well as the degree to which models in general had evolved all contribute to their complexity. Florence Nightingale was concerned with establishing a training for nurses while Virginia Henderson (1972), whose model also reflects a predominant physiological base, developed Florence Nightingale's thinking much further. It would seem that with Hildegard Peplau's more psychologically based model these form the main building blocks on which the third and fourth generation of nurses and theoreticians have built.

Evolution is about adaptation to the environment, so each new model not only reflects aspects of this, for instance the politicoeconomic aspects which greatly influence the activities of living, but also shows a greater awareness and understanding of life and the effects that illness and injury may have on all aspects of it. Perhaps one feature which nurses have yet to come to terms with in so far as nursing is concerned is that of sexuality. Like the seemingly new interest in the politicoeconomic effects on health, expression of one's sexuality has been of paramount importance from time immemorial.

Fundamental parts of a model

In discussing nursing models so far, an attempt has been made to define a model and to note the difficulties in so doing. In addition three types of model have been identified and examples of each described. All nursing models have certain fundamental parts, but unfortunately, since the literature on models spans both sides of the Atlantic, so too does the terminology. In essence, the main features which are identified in the British literature describe a nursing model in the following terms.

1. The goal of nursing.
2. A definition of the client or patient.
3. The role of nursing.
4. The source of difficulty for the client or patient.
5. The focus of intervention.

6. The mode of intervention.
7. The desired outcome.

American literature describes the elements of a nursing model using the essential ingredients of prescriptive theories as follows.

1. Goal-content – specified as the aim for the activity.
2. Prescriptions – actions to realize the goal content.
3. A survey list – which serves as a supplement to present actions and a preparation for future prescriptions.

The goal content is naturally concerned with the situation to be produced, since it is based in a situation-producing theoretical framework and therefore identifies and describes the features of this. For instance the goal content of the Orem self-care model (1971) is to assist man to achieve health and to develop an optimal level of self care.

The prescriptions describe the types of activities that will produce the desired outcome. Orem is very specific about these – acting for or doing for another; guiding another; supporting another (physically or psychologically); providing an environment that promotes personal development in relation to becoming able to meet present or future demands of action; and teaching another. Since this model is based on an assumption that the patient is willing and able to become self-caring, Orem further identifies the level of assistance that the nurse should consider. She describes these as wholly compensatory, partially compensatory, and educative-supportive. These three types of nursing system reflect the level of assistance required by the patient.

The survey list serves as a supplement to the goal content and the prescriptions. It encompasses the following features about the activity.

1. Agency – who is involved in the activity.
2. Patiency – who receives this activity.
3. Framework – where the activity is performed.
4. Terminus – what is the end point.
5. Procedure – how the activity is organized.
6. Dynamics – what is the energy source for the activity.

Orem states that both the nurse and the patient are involved in the activity; they are agents. The activity of the nurse varies with the level of assistance required by the patient and the ultimate goal of the patient in becoming self-caring. The nurse, however, is the designer and controller of the nursing station.

The patiency–recipient of the activity is always man. In Orem's model man is described as having self-care demands that he cannot meet himself.

The framework in this survey is only concerned with where the activity occurs. Each model clarifies this although they generally do not set limitations and for instance Orem suggests only that the activity may take place 'wherever the goal can be realized'.

The terminus is a direct reflection of whether the goal has been achieved, so in respect of Orem's model she describes it as a point when the patient is optimally self-caring to the extent that it is possible with nursing assistance.

Most American models use a nursing procedure, but adopt a different terminology in some instances. Orem identifies the stage as follows.

1. Determining why the person needs nursing care – what are the therapeutic self-care demands that are not being met.
2. Planning a system of care in which the patient is enabled to become self-caring.
3. Implementing the care by initiating, conducting and controlling 'assisting action' towards the achievement of the goal.

The dynamics of the activity are concerned with the nurse and patient, but specifically in relation to what they each have to bring to the situation. Orem suggests the nurse contributes her knowledge of, for instance the physical, psychological and mechanical factors which will influence how care is given and the patient affects the situation by his motivation, interest and abilities to achieve the goal.

Models and practice

Johnson's definition of a nursing model is 'a systematically constructed, scientifically based and logically related set of concepts which identify the essential components of nursing practice together with the theoretical bases for these concepts and the values required in their use by the practitioner'. In order to put the model into practice, nurses also need a systematic approach. This is possible by using the nursing process in conjunction with an appropriate nursing model.

Nursing process
Unlike nursing models, the nursing process involves not only intellectual skills, but also skills in decision making, observation and interpersonal relationships.

It may be described as a problem solving-approach to nursing, which involves interaction with the patient, making decisions and carrying out nursing actions, based on an assessment of an individual patient's situation. It is cyclical in nature.

Assessment of patient problems
The assessment stage involves taking a nursing history using an appropriate model as a framework. Here the nurse in conjunction with the patient assesses the patient's needs and identifies problems which can be alleviated by nursing care.

Planning patient care.
Following the assessment phase the patient's nursing care can then be appropriately planned in relation to each identified problem, by setting goals which also reflect the patient's values, beliefs and a positive lifestyle. These goals will be evaluated in relation to the expected outcome of the

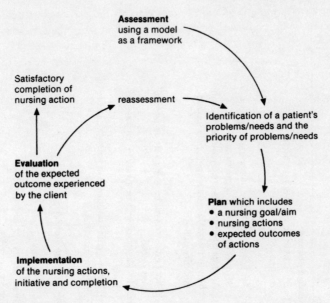

Fig. 2.5 The nursing process

nursing action. Table 2.1 is an example of a problem, identified on the first day following admission of a patient who has had a cerebro-vascular accident.

The nurse has to make some decisions not only about the problems which have been identified by the patient but also about potential problems which she is aware may occur either because of the nature of the disease process or injury or its effect on the person's biopsychosocial well being, or because of intervention by medical and other staff.

Implementation
Subsequent nursing actions will include both doing things for and with the patient as well as teaching and listening to him.

Evaluation. Appraisal of the outcome is a most important step, representing the satisfactory conclusion of nursing care, or of reassessment when the expected outcome has not been achieved or has been ineffective in relation to the patient's problem. An evaluation of the expected outcome is also found in Table 2.1.

Nursing process and nursing models

The nursing process is clearly about attempting to meet patients' needs – unmet needs are problems. Some nursing models, for example Henderson and Roper, are formulated around Maslow's theory of needs (1954). Like the theories already described Maslow's theory itself is hierarchical and sometimes depicted as a pyramid in which man's basic physiological needs and values, food, drink, sex

Table 2.1 Care plan for Mr Lawrence

Problem	Action	Expected outcome
Not able to walk because of weakness down left side of body	(i) Allow Mr Lawrence to express his feelings.	(i) Mr Lawrence will begin to accept his condition.
	(ii) Encourage him to acknowledge his left side at all times.	(ii) Mr Lawrence will be increasingly aware of his left side and how it is positioned.
	(iii) Discuss exercises with him and physiotherapist	(iii) Appropriate exercises are identified to enable him to maintain muscle tone, balance and mobility in bed.
Goal		
To walk around flat safely	(iv) Assist him to do exercises twice per shift.	(iv) Mr Lawrence will be able to sit up and roll over in bed.
	(v) Teach and encourage wife to do same while visiting.	(v) Mrs Lawrence will be aware of his physical abilities.
	(vi) Assist him to sit on edge of bed with minimum support.	(vi) He will gain confidence in balance and use of appropriate muscles.

Evaluation

(i) Mr Lawrence has been tearful and showed signs of frustration when not able to sit up alone.

(ii) Seems unaware of left arm. Experienced cramp pain in calf of left leg.

(iii) Exercises explained to Mr Lawrence by physiotherapist.

(iv) Not able to do exercises without supervision. Able to raise left arm above head when right arm used.

(v) Mrs Lawrence spent four hours with husband and assisted him with arm and leg exercises.

(vi) Mr Lawrence sat on edge of bed supported by nurse on left side.

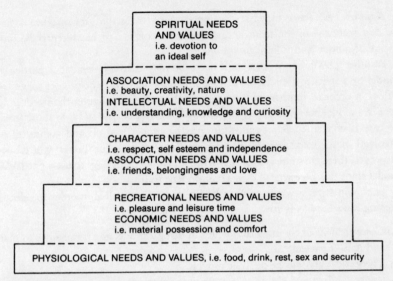

Fig. 2.6 Adapted from Maslow's hierarchy of human needs and values in the pursuit of self actualization.

and security form the building blocks in the ultimate pursuit of self-realization (see Fig. 2.6).

Maslow's theory is one aspect of the Roper model of nursing and helps the nurse to focus on relevant factors and to formulate priorities in relation to problems. It states that only after ensuring that the needs and values at the base of the pyramid are met to the patient's satisfaction and to a state that maintains his personal well-being, will it be appropriate to focus on those needs higher up the pyramid. As part of a model therefore it clarifies the nurse's thinking about her own nursing practice.

However as Fig. 2.2 shows, a model is formulated by writing a number of concepts into a coherent whole which is also able to be implemented in practice. Two other aspects which are implicit in a nursing model are concerned with the assumptions on which the model is based and the values which are emphasized. In deciding which model to use as a framework for assessing a patient it is important therefore to analyse it and to consider whether the assumptions, values, concepts and their relationships are in fact the ones which would best serve the interests of the patient and the nurse in planning care.

NURSING MODELS IN CLINICAL SETTINGS

Criteria for selecting a nursing model in a clinical area
In deciding to select a particular nursing model for a clinical area, it is important in preliminary discussions to identify the features of the present circumstances.

A number of factors may have prompted these discussions, for instance it may be that someone in the team is undertaking a course and has recently become aware of models and is keen to use one.

Another possibility is that staff have been told to implement a particular model by a specific date. In either case it is possible to use the process suggested below in order to implement a model – in the first case however the freedom to choose a model may prove to be more rewarding, not only in so far as the delivery of care is concerned but because the process of negotiation and commitment involved in the selection will have made the staff function better as a group. However, there are some advantages when an authority decides to use a particular model since this necessitates their commitment to it.

The main criteria which need to be satisfactorily fulfilled in order to select a nursing model are as follows.

1. Commitment of the staff to the idea of using a model as a framework to plan and deliver patient care.
2. Theoretical knowledge of some models.
3. Understanding and ability to use the nursing process.
4. Support by management and teaching staff.
5. Learner preparation.
6. Patient preparation.
7. Medical staff preparation.
8. Documentation.

1. Commitment

Commitment is defined as 'engagement or involvement that restricts freedom of action'. It involves negotiation from a position of strength. Commitment in this sense therefore involves being and feeling part of the group which is making investigations to select a model. This necessitates being available to participate in meetings that will occur on a regular basis. The group itself needs to be comprised of all grades of permanent staff who will be involved or affected by the change.

Occasionally one or two representatives will need to be willing to talk with groups outside the particular clinical area. For instance at Sisters' meetings, assessors' meetings, to students and medical staff about the intentions of the group, and to make progress reports. Likewise it may be helpful while dealing with a specific subject to invite particular people into the group for a period of time.

Each meeting needs a chairperson, an agenda and a definite start and finish time. By setting these boundaries the group takes on a definite role and begins to develop a sense of purpose. From this firm base excursions into the unknown may be made both in terms of knowledge and terms of relationships. Brief notes of the main topics discussed and the actions agreed and by whom are helpful. It is useful if all group members take on this task at some time.

Having gained a commitment to establish a working party it is helpful to set some deadlines; these, if reasonably able to be met, focus attention on the purpose and if not, provide good experience for the group in justifying the need for an extension – both to themselves and to others.

Earlier it was suggested that preliminary meetings should identify the features of the present position; they also need to establish levels of expertise both in using models and the nursing process, as well as the means to improve and extend them.

In considering the present, it is important to reflect on the past and to consider possible changes – both at ward level and in the wider sense. What does each member of the group bring with them to assist in this task? Varying degrees of knowledge, skills and attitudes. It is important to recognize that the chairperson is not necessarily the best equipped in so far as knowledge and skills are concerned, but that he/she has the capacity to encourage individuals to recognize their own strengths and weaknesses so that a realistic appraisal by the group of what they know and what they need help with, is made at this early stage.

There may be a veritable Aladdin's Cave! Whatever emerges from these discussions, the group needs a certain level of knowledge and understanding about models in general and about how to use one, having decided it would make a contribution to patient care.

2. Theoretical knowledge of models
A School of Nursing library can be a fairly uninviting source of information especially when at best there is no librarian to assist the tentative user and at worst there is one but nursing models mean fossilized brains! This need not be a deterrent. It is possible to find a wealth of information in libraries and quite easily. If the nearest library does not have a librarian, find out one that does and discuss with the librarian what the needs of the group are. There is an increasing number of British books on models as well as many American ones. These may well be on the shelves or can be borrowed from other libraries.

Another very useful source of up to date information are the Nursing Indices, for example *Nursing Bibliography*, published monthly by the RCN, and *International Nursing Index*, published quarterly by the American Journal of Nursing. Current American and British nursing journals may be useful both from the theoretical and clinical standpoints.

If it is more convenient to use a nonstaffed library, find the catalogue of the books and assess if there are some which seem appropriate as well as reasonably recent. If this is not a fruitful quest, it may be more beneficial to visit a public library, which will have catalogues of all books currently in print and which can obtain those you need for a small fee.

Apart from a good library and a good librarian, there are several other sources that can be tapped. For example, nurse managers will know of staff who have either attended courses and study days or been on visits to hospitals using a model of the nursing process, with whom some discussions might take place. Models are increasingly being introduced into the basic curriculum of nurses in training, so many tutors are familiar with them and may be willing to support a group in selecting and implementing one. A clinical teacher, or practical work teacher working in the area might be usefully invited to join the group, as well as to support trained staff and learners during the process of change. Finally, some post basic education departments compile a register of research projects and innovations from within the district. This may well include details of similar projects.

The suggestions so far cost time, those which follow also involve some financial outlay. It may be valuable for some members of the group to attend workshops on the nursing process and models and to visit clinical areas which have implemented change. Details of these are published in many nursing journals. More senior nurses are increasingly being encouraged to participate in ENB Course 998, as further preparation for their roles as teachers and assessors in clinical settings. This course and the course 'Developments in Nursing Care', for both general and psychiatric nurses, include an introduction to nursing models, as do the London Diploma in Nursing, the CNAA Diploma in Professional Nursing Studies and degree courses in nursing.

3. Understanding and ability to use the nursing process

The ability to use the nursing process as well as having a good working knowledge of models is important for both learner and trained nursing staff. It is in the context of developing the skills that are necessary in order to do this, that tutorial staff may be of most help and support. A lack of the skills required to implement the nursing process seems especially to hinder the introduction of a model of nursing.

4. Support by management and teaching staff

Tutorial and management staff can assist in developing not only the intellectual skills, but also skills in decision-making, observation and inter-personal relationships. They can support and encourage staff during the process of learning and evaluation. The process may seem quite slow and requires the encouragement of someone less involved in it, to stimulate and reinforce the achievements that have already been made.

A more formal way in which the working knowledge required by members of the group may be achieved is by means of a contract. Like other contracts, for example, when buying a house, it is essentially between two people, both of whom contract to ensure that a mutually agreed goal is achieved in a particular period of time. By negotiating a goal which will be achieved by carefully planned objectives, the individual is enabled to develop skills and knowledge in areas in which he/she feels less confident, within the bounds of a positive relationship in which the means to achieve them has been clearly identified. For example a member of the group may wish to develop her decision-making skills.

The objectives which are finally agreed on with the contractor will reflect the current and the desired knowledge and skills. The contract could have of the following features.

1. Identify the main features involved in decision making.
2. Describe briefly the fundamental differences between three approaches to decision making.
3. Describe a current situation and suggest two alternatives to the process of decision making.
4. Demonstrate one approach in decision making.
5. Evaluate the first four parts of the contract.

The value of such a contract is not only explicit, in that it assists the nurse to acquire the knowledge and skills she believes she lacks, but through the process of the contract she is encouraged at each stage to develop decision-making skills herself. The nurse can specifically be helped to do this by assisting her in choosing relevant learning strategies and resources.

Contract learning can be a valuable experience not only for the 'learner' but also for the person with whom the contract is made, because he/she also agrees to give time and effort that will assist the 'learner' to obtain the mutually agreed objectives. In this process the 'teacher' will also learn. One of the many useful spin-offs for the teacher is not only acting as a facilitator but also becoming very aware of the reality of implementing the nursing process.

5. Learner preparation

Any attempt to select a model and use it in conjunction with the nursing process involves the knowledge and skills to do this oneself, but also the ability and willingness to transmit this in one's everyday work as well as when specifically with learners. As has been discussed elsewhere, only by establishing the learner's knowledge and skills through discussion and observation of her delivery of care to patients will it be possible to assist the learner to develop her current level and further it in a particular direction.

6. Patient participation

To what extent is it reasonable or important to consider patients participating in the selection of a model? To some extent this will vary with the degree to which patients contribute to their own assessments and plans. This in turn depends on the nature of the patients' problems. For example, it is less time-consuming and gives the patient a sense of control over his immediate situation if he is asked to complete as much of the assessment as he can, either on the actual form or a piece of paper (whichever seems appropriate). This may take place prior to admission. Assessment forms (sent out with information on how to complete them) may be included in the letter advising of admission, or they can be completed on admission with perhaps the help of a close friend or relative if this seems appropriate to the patient. This can then form the basis of a discussion with a nurse. This approach can be considered for routine admissions especially short stay admissions, as well as readmissions.

There are a number of aspects which need to be considered when seeking the patient's participation in the selection of a model. These include physical condition, psychological state and social and intellectual factors. For example, are the factors which the model is based upon useful to the patient as a means of helping him to clarify his problems? Or are they open to misinterpretation; loaded with personal values and assumptions; using concepts that are understood only by those with the necessary professional jargon? Does the physical size, colour and layout of the form encourage the patient to make meaningful responses or expected responses?

Patients will respond to pilot assessment forms in many ways – many however will be pleased when a nurse asks them for their comments on its usefulness to ensuring their care is individualized and if improvements might be made.

7. Medical staff preparation

One of the competencies identified in the Nurses, Midwives and Health Visitors Act 1979 states that in order to become registered a nurse is required to 'work in a team with other nurses and with medical and paramedical staff and social workers'. Another of the competencies states she is required to 'devise a plan of nursing care based on the assessment with the co-operation of the patient, to the extent that this is possible taking into account the medical prescription'. Yet another competency states she should 'implement the planned programme of nursing care and where appropriate teach and co-ordinate other members in the caring team who may be responsible for implementing specific aspects of the nursing care'.

One group of people which each of these competencies is referring to is the medical staff. In terms of our respective histories we both have long ones; in terms of viewing ourselves as members of a professional body, nurses have some catching up to do.

It would seem that one area in which the nurse can do this in relation to the medical staff is through experiences that involve each developing the knowledge and confidence to really talk with the other – in the firm belief that each has a valid contribution to make to patient care. Confidence and 'arrogance' have an unfortunate habit of becoming entwined – confidence is based on trust and involves a willingness to be open with others; arrogance occurs when a person claims something unjustly to or for themselves, is presumptuous, overbearing, does not hear what is said.

Generally a person 'does not hear what is said' because for some reason this poses a threat to their personal being, status or role. As a result he or she builds a defence, that is metaphorically builds a wall between the threat and herself. Both nurses and medical staff can be confident and arrogant. To encourage confidence the nurse has to learn to trust herself and her ability and that of the people with whom she works. This may involve hearing criticism as well as praise, and being able to recognize the true weight of each.

In respect of arrogance, it is useful to reflect why this behaviour occurs – Where does the threat come from? What is it actually striking – pride, ignorance, the need to be in control or an inability to express or even accept feelings of anxiety, doubt and uncertainty about the situation?

At one level the nurse has a statutory duty to provide care taking into account the medical prescription; at another she is required to work in a team with medical staff and at another she has a duty to teach others. In the widest sense of teaching, therefore, she needs to help medical staff firstly understand why she feels a nursing model may be useful and secondly to ensure their comments will be welcomed in relation to the specific model the nursing staff choose and perhaps even to encourage medical staff to review their own model in the light of the chosen nursing model so that each forms a useful and valuable framework around which to plan care.

8. Documentation

The last factor which needs consideration when selecting a model is the format of the documentation. Prior to the advent of the nursing process and models, and the documentation this involves, nurses were considered less harshly in the eyes of the law. Drawing up an assessment form which reflects the main components of a model is only a small part of the process, although a fundamental one.

It is also imperative that any changes are documented and discussed not only with senior nursing staff because of policy, financial and legal implications involved, but are also tried out over a period of time (for example three months) at the end of which any changes that are deemed necessary by the working party as the result of all the staff experiences, are made.

Another useful pilot experience is for learners to be encouraged to use the model in the classroom – this encourages both their decision-making and interpersonal skills – but the degree of ease or difficulty they experience may be a valuable indication of the relative amount of help qualified staff will need to use it in their clinical area.

Introducing a model into patient care

This section builds on negotiation skills that will have evolved during the selection of an appropriate model for a patient care setting. However, prior to outlining how this might take place, some attention will be given to the situation in which the staff have been told to implement a particular model by a specific date. Usually this arises because a particular hospital or unit has decided that some sort of standard organization of patient documentation is required, and a working party of different grades of trained staff, often from a variety of specialist areas, go through a process similar to that described earlier.

In terms of hospital policies, the financial cost of printing forms and of all staff being familiar with the process, the introduction of one model for a multi-specialist organization, e.g. a district general hospital, makes good sense. However, it may be that such a model is in fact not very appropriate for different groups of patients, e.g. acutely disturbed psychiatric patients, maternity patients, children, long term psychogeriatric patients and mentally handicapped people.

A model is only a framework, it cannot provide the care. It can however encourage the nurse to consider dimensions of care which might not otherwise be systematically considered and in so doing improve the potential quality of care. Perhaps then the implementation of a district model needs to be tested out and like a theory refuted when necessary, so that a modified version emerges when appropriate that can serve the needs of both the patient and staff well.

The main aspects that need to be especially considered when actually implementing a model are:

1. Trained staff preparation.
2. Learner preparation.
3. Managing the change.
4. Evaluation and review of the change.
5. Future place.

1. Trained staff preparation

As the result of the working party's discussions on levels of knowledge and skills in relation to models and the nursing process, it is possible to arrive at a programme which will reflect the needs of the staff and enable a decision to be made about which model to try. The milestones which have to be achieved in due course are a transformation of the theory into an assessment format which also reflects the ultimate goal of the model.

A good understanding of the model, its advantages, disadvantages and limitations is essential in order that the staff can translate these into a manageable, logical and systematic format. This can usefully be tried out by students in the classroom, students assessing patients in a clinical situation under supervision and the trained staff in the group, assessing patients in the particular area – for a short period after which a review is made.

The usefulness of the model can be identified most objectively by having some 'control' – patients whose care is given by trained staff and students using the ward's current documentation and comparing patients with similar conditions whose care has been planned following assessment using the new model.

A second aspect of the review and staff preparation at this stage will involve anyone who has done an assessment using the new model since the review must include an analysis of the layout, use of the concepts and ease with which all staff have found in using it. It may be necessary to have another pilot study if several factors are changed. However, once the final format of the assessment documentation is agreed by the group it must then be discussed with the rest of the staff in the area who will be using it. It is most important they are given time not only to understand the theory on which it is based and the rationale for its use but also express their feelings about the changes.

2. Learner preparation

Learner preparation can be done in a number of ways. If the model is to be implemented throughout the district learners will receive training not only in the nursing process, but also about the particular model in the school, which will be gradually reinforced during each experience. The example of a clinical supervisor or mentor can be invaluable not only in helping learners to make the links between theory and practice but also in developing the skills which are an integral part of the process of learning to use a model – whether this is used throughout the district or in a particular area.

As the learner gains in experience and is given feedback on her assessments of less ill patients, so her confidence in her own ability to assess more difficult patients will develop and become a reality. The mentor can then encourage the learner to become more reflective about the process and outcomes herself.

3. Managing the change

Much has been written and is being done to help people in all walks of life to manage change. In introducing a new model to a clinical setting the effects of change will be as various as the people involved. The way it is managed will affect the outcome of the experience. There are a number of concrete factors which will assist in making it a positive experience. Ultimately however it will depend on how individuals feel about how it is affecting them.

The ward staff need to agree on a timescale for implementing the model. Those who have not been involved in the working group may feel they would like a different timescale – for a number of reasons – not least because they are less familiar with the model than those who have been working with it quite intensely for some time. Agreeing on a timescale should involve not only deciding on a specific date to start, but also whether every patient will have an assessment using the model or perhaps initially certain types of patient. It should involve the designing of a teaching programme for all new staff including learners to ensure that each has the relevant knowledge, understanding and supervision to make an assessment using the model, and the identification of clinical supervisors to do this.

In particular, time needs to be set aside each week to encourage staff to express their feelings about using the model – this requires an especially sensitive facilitator, so that feelings can be expressed and the staff are encouraged to accept what is being said and to support each other, through what may be quite a stressful experience. Two final points which usefully focus energy and motivate different members of the group are to write up the experience – the profits from which can very justifiably be used to have a celebration.

It is not only important but valuable for a review to be made of the change once it has been operational for some time. Much of what has been said in the latter part of this chapter has laid particular emphasis on developing the necessary expertise to make an assessment of a patient based on a particular model. However, in reality, by introducing a new model it is anticipated that the care patients receive will be more appropriate, of a good standard and aimed at achieving a particular goal. Evaluating the outcome of this is therefore essential and may usefully be carried out by service managers using a number of parameters measuring standard of care, patients' declared satisfaction with their care, including effects on the budget, staff satisfaction (sickness and absence rates) and learner evaluation of the clinical environment – including assessments taken and passed and/or outcomes of continuous assessment. These should be discussed with the ward staff and give useful confirmation of the values of the change.

5. Future plans

Introducing a new model into a clinical area is a major venture. Nevertheless at this stage it is worthwhile to consider a number of directions for future developments. The most positive will be to continue with the model. However, a broad evaluation such as that just described may also lead to one of a number of alternative suggestions. To use a different model would require enormous energy and motivation, as well as having educational and financial implications. Likewise the use of two or three models in a clinical setting where there are patients with very different needs is a possibility, but a tremendous undertaking; using some key factors from different existing models may be more appropriate and manageable or alternatively designing one to suit the needs of the patient and staff.

Change affects people differently – some people respond to the challenge, others find the personal and professional adjustments unsettling and anxiety-provoking. A balance is needed in which staff feel able to make suggestions that will enhance their personal satisfaction with work and also maintain the standard of care they offer and give to the patients. This may be unsettling and anxiety-provoking for some, since keeping up to date with changes in the education of nurses and in clinical practice demands a certain commitment – not least in time. However, a change has also to outweigh the energy required to implement it. Change has to be more useful than whatever it is replacing.

CONCLUSIONS

The first part of this chapter was concerned with clarifying some of the terms commonly used in nursing theory – both in this country and America. In the process an attempt was made to give an overview of some American models as well as a much-used British model. The intention was to familiarize the reader with some of the many concepts used, in an attempt to whet the appetite for a more in-depth search for a model that would serve the needs of her patients and colleagues better than a current assessment format. The implications of such a search are more far-reaching and will affect all those involved in the change.

Implementing a model has been the explicit aim of the latter part of this chapter and an attempt has been made to suggest how this could be managed, acknowledged and rewarded as well as identifying difficulties and how they might be minimized or at least foreseen.

The competencies demand that enrolled nurses assist in giving care and that registered nurses take the responsibility for the care which is given, using the nursing process. This is only possible in the professional sense if it occurs within the framework of the appropriate model. In order to make this a reality, nurses therefore need to be equipped with skills in observation, decision-making, interpersonal relationships and the practical delivery of care. They need the knowledge on which to base these skills. In the process of gaining this synthesis nurses need above all to develop the inherent ability to be exploratory and curious and must be allowed to be creative with the choices that are available to them and supported and encouraged to pursue these.

TOPICS FOR DISCUSSION

1. To what extent does Roper's model fulfil the elements of a model that are identified in this chapter?
2. The nurse's role in Roy's adaptation model is to modify the stimuli which are affecting adaptation. How might she be helped to do this in the example given in the chapter?
3. Orem's self-care model advocates health education as a major nursing role. To what extent is this necessary and desirable in your clinical practice?
4. Peplau's model was formulated in the early 1950s in a mental health environment when the nurse's role as well as her educational experiences were drawn from a narrower perspective. To what extent does it serve a useful purpose today?
5. How are the patients for whom you care enabled to express their sexuality? Discuss how learners may be encouraged to accept this activity of living as part of a patient's life and why they may be reluctant to do so.
6. A model is only a tool – how can you justify its use to an unconvinced colleague?

REFERENCES AND SOURCES

Aggleton, P. and Chalmers, H. (1987). 'Models of nursing, nursing practice and nurse education', *Journal of Advanced Nursing* **12**: 573–81.
Aspinall, M. J. (1981). *Decision Making For Patient Care: Applying the Nursing Process.* New York: Appleton-Century-Croft; Hemel Hempstead: Prentice Hall.
Bailey, J. T. and Claus, K. E. (1975). *Decision Making in Nursing: Tools for Change.* St Louis: C. V. Mosby.
Bickerton, J. *et al.* (1979). *Nursing: Theory and Practice.* London: McGraw Hill.
Blondis, M. N. and Jackson, B. E. (1982). *Non-verbal Communication with Patients: Back to the Human Touch.* Chichester: Wiley.

Boore, J. R. P. (1978). *Prescription For Recovery.* London: Royal College of Nursing.

Bridge, W. and MacCleod Clark, J. (eds) (1981). *Communication in Nursing Care.* London: H. M. & M. Publishers.

Calman, J. (1983). *Talking With Patients: A Guide To Good Practice.* London: Heinemann Medical.

Carnevali, D. L. (1983). *Nursing Care Planning: Diagnosis and Management.* London: Lippincott.

Chinn, P. L. and Jacobs, M. K. (1983). *Theory and Nursing: A Systematic Approach.* St Louis: C. V. Mosby.

Clark, C. C. (1977). *The Nurse As Group Leader.* New York: Springer.

Cooley, C. (1909). *Human Nature and Social Order.* Glencoe: Free Press.

Crow, J. (1980). *Effects of Preparation on Problem Solving: An Investigation into Student Nurses and their Ability to Identify Problems and to Suggest Nursing Interventions.* London: Macmillan Journals.

Dickoff, J. and James, P. (1968). 'A Theory of Theories: A Position Paper', *Nursing Research* 17: 197–203.

Faulkner, A. (1984). *Communication.* Edinburgh: Churchill-Livingstone.

Faulkner, A. (1985). *Nursing: A Creative Approach.* Eastbourne: Balliere Tindall.

Fawcett, J. (1984). *Analysis and Evaluation of Conceptual Models of Nursing.* Philadelphia: F. A. Davis.

Fitzpatrick, J. J. and Whall, A. L. (eds) (1983). *Conceptual Models of Nursing: Analysis and Application.* Bowie (Maryland): Brady.

Ford, J. A. G. *et al.* (1979). *Applied Decision Making For Nurses.* St Louis: C. V. Mosby.

Goldstone, L. A. *et al.* (1983). *Monitor: An Index of the Quality of Nursing Care For Acute Medical and Surgical Wards.* Newcastle-Upon-Tyne: Polytechnic Products Ltd.

Griffin, J. W. and Christensen, P. J. (1982). *Nursing Process: Application of Theories Frameworks and Models.* St Louis: C. V. Mosby.

Hayward, J. (1975). *Information – a Prescription Against Pain.* London: Royal College of Nursing.

Henderson, V. (1972). *Basic Principles of Nursing Care.* Geneva: International Council of Nursing.

Johnson, D. (1980). 'The behavioural system model for nursing' in *Conceptual Models For Nursing Practice,* J. P. Riehl and C. Roy (eds). New York: Appleton-Century-Crofts.

Kershaw, B. and Savage, J. (eds) (1986). *Models for Nursing.* Chichester: Wiley.

King, I. M. (1981). *A Theory For Nursing: Systems, Concepts, Process.* Chichester: Wiley.

Kratz, C. R. (1978). *Care of the Long-term Sick in the Community.* Edinburgh: Churchill-Livingstone.

Kratz, C. R. (ed.) (1979). *The Nursing Process.* London: Balliere Tindall.

Leggett, P. A. (1987). *Help for Quality: Patient Care Audit.* Poole General Hospital.

McFarlane, E. A. (1980). 'Nursing theory: the comparison of four theoretical models', *Journal of Advanced Nursing* 5: 3–19.

Marriner, A. (1979). *The Nursing Process: A Scientific Approach to Nursing Care.* St Louis: C. V. Mosby.

Maslow, A. H. (1954). *Motivation and Personality.* London: Methuen.

McFarlane of Llandaff and Castledine, G. (1982). *A Guide to the Practice of Nursing Using the Nursing Process.* St Louis: C. V. Mosby.

Murphy, J. (1971). *Theoretical Issues in Professional Nursing.* New York: Wiley.

Nightingale, F. (1970). *Notes on Nursing: What It Is and What It Is Not.* London: Duckworth.

Nursing Theories Conference Group (1980). *Nursing Theories: The Base for Professional Nursing Practice.* Englewood Cliffs: Prentice Hall Inc.

Orem, D. E. (1983). *Nursing: Concepts of Practice*. New York: McGraw Hill.

Pearson, A. and Vaughan, B. (1986). *Nursing Models for Practice*. London: Heinemann.

Peplau, H. (1952). *Interpersonal Relationships in Nursing*. New York: Pitman.

Popper, K. (1972). *Conjectures and Refutations: The Growth of Scientific Knowledge*. London: Routledge and Kegan Paul.

Porritt, L. (1984). *Communication: Choices for Nurses*. Edinburgh:Churchill-Livingstone.

Riehl, J. and Roy, C. (eds) (1980). *Conceptual Models for Nursing Practice*. New York: Appleton-Century-Crofts and Hemel Hempstead: Prentice Hall.

Roper, N., Logan, W. W. and Tierney, A. J. (1981). *Learning to Use the Nursing Process*. Edinburgh: Churchill-Livingstone.

Roper, N., Logan, W. W. and Tierney, A. J. (1982). *Principles of Nursing*. Edinburgh: Churchill-Livingstone.

Roper, N., Logan, W. W. and Tierney, A. J. (1985). *The Elements of Nursing*. Edinburgh: Churchill-Livingstone.

Roy, C. (ed.) (1984). *Introduction to Nursing: An Adaptation Model*. Englewood Cliffs: Prentice Hall Inc.

Stevens, B. J. (1984). *Nursing Theory: Analysis, Application, Evaluation*. Boston: Little, Brown.

Willis, L. D. (ed.) (1984). *Measuring the Quality of Care*. Edinburgh: Churchill-Livingstone.

Wright, S. G. (1986). *Building and Using a Model in Nursing*. London: Edward Arnold.

Yura, H. (1978). *The Nursing Process: Assessing, Planning, Implementing and Evaluating*. New York: Appleton-Century-Croft and Hemel Hempstead: Prentice Hall.

Yura, H. and Walsh, M. B. (eds) (1983). *Human Needs 3 and Nursing Process*. New York: Appleton-Century-Croft.

CHAPTER THREE

EDUCATING ADULTS

INTRODUCTION

The nursing profession has long valued the attributes of maturity and personal responsibility in its members, but as shown in Chapter One, nurse training has often failed to respond to these characteristics in its students. This chapter is based on the assumption that nursing students, whether in initial or post-initial training, have a legitimate claim to an education responsive to their needs as adult learners.

In recent years the growth of continuing and adult education available to the public has stimulated many theorists, researchers and adult educators to consider the unique characteristics and needs of adult learners. This chapter considers four contributions to our understanding of teaching and learning. These approaches are taken as representative of a wide range of theories and each is presented in summary form as a paradigm case. The implications for nurse education and clinical supervisors of each are then considered. It is not intended to be an exhaustive account of the field, but rather a selective review which seeks to support and inform the work of clinical supervisors.

The chapter concludes with consideration of the kind of nurse demanded for practice in the 1990s and beyond and with a proposed eclectic framework to serve as guidance to clinical supervisors.

Defining teaching, learning and education

Learning is an inordinately complex phenomenon and has long been studied by psychologists and others. Unfortunately for readers of a text such as this, there seems to be no adequate theory to account for all aspects of learning.

Learning has been defined as 'a relatively permanent change in behaviour that occurs as the result of prior experience' (Hilgard et al., 1975). However, Jarvis (1983a) notes that the 'acquisition of new knowledge need not result in behavioural change, but learning has occurred'. He proposes the definition that learning is 'the acquisition of knowledge, skill or attitude by study, experience or teaching' (Jarvis, 1983b). Note here the three elements commonly regarded as interrelated yet independent (see Figure 3.1). Knowledge, skills and attitudes are all generally accepted as being subject to development. Some forms of learning will result predominantly in skill enhancement, some predominantly in knowledge development and some in attitude change.

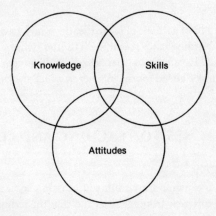

Fig. 3.1 Learning domains

Teaching, the process by which one person brings about learning in another, is not essential to learning. Many learners acquire knowledge, skills or attitudes independent of any formal teaching. Self-directed learning accounts for much learning in adult life and should not be underestimated. From research undertaken by Tough (1971) and others it is apparent that learning in adulthood is very common and that most is self-motivated and planned by the learner (Moore, 1984).

This is not to say that teaching is irrelevant or unimportant in adult learning but that, given certain conditions, most adults engage in much more learning than is often acknowledged. Having said this, can such learning be regarded as education? Education has been defined by Jarvis (1983b) as 'any planned series of incidents having a humanistic basis, directed towards the participant(s') learning and understanding'. Tough's (1971) research suggests that self-directed or independent learning meets the criteria in Jarvis's definition and we may therefore conclude that education may result both from teaching or from independent study.

In summary then, the acquisition of knowledge, skill or attitude can occur through study, experience or teaching and may be construed as education if it has occurred as a result of a planned series of incidents which have a humanistic basis. Learning and education can be self-directed or facilitated by a teacher. In this chapter we are concerned with both learning and teaching within the context of an educational process. For our purpose here contributions to the understanding of learning and teaching will be reviewed within a framework which acknowledges the following points.

1. That education is deliberate, planned, organized and undertaken with the conscious intention of changing knowledge, skills or attitudes. (Moore, 1984).
2. That this process involves pre-active, interactive and evaluative phases. (Stones, 1979).

What follows is a brief account of some theories which have contributed to our understanding of learning and teaching. Theories which comprise the four approaches identified have been so categorized for illustrative purposes only. No philosophical rigour is claimed for the manner in which these categories have been established.

FOUR APPROACHES TO TEACHING AND LEARNING

The theory of andragogy

Malcolm Knowles, a contemporary adult educator, has argued that adult learners are psychologically different from children and that the techniques used by adult educators should therefore be different from those of teachers of children. Knowles has coined the term andragogy to refer to this theory implying that it is the 'art and science of helping adults learn' as distinct from pedagogy, 'the art and science of teaching children' (Knowles, 1985). Knowles identifies five areas in which he believes adults can be shown to be unique as learners, and draws attention to the implications of these assumptions for the educational process (Knowles, 1970).

1. *Self concept.* Knowles argues that the learner moves from dependence to independence during maturation. Children rely on adults to decide how, when and what they learn, whereas adults are self-directing and responsible for their own actions. The implications of this assumption are as follows:

(a) The physical and psychological climate in which learning is to occur should be informal and engender acceptance, respect, support and maturity.
(b) Emphasis should be placed on self-diagnosis of learning needs involving a definition of the competencies to be acquired as an amalgam of the student's and the teacher's expectations; an assessment of the student's present level of competence is made and the student is helped to identify gaps between his present level of competence and the level of competence to be achieved. Dissatisfaction about the gap and a sense of direction and self-improvement are encouraged.
(c) The student is encouraged to participate with the teacher in planning the learning experience. This involves translating diagnosed needs into specific educational objectives or goals and designing experiences to achieve these goals.
(d) The teaching-learning transaction is a mutual responsibility between teacher and student and where appropriate responsibility for helping others to learn is shared within small groups.

(e) The giving of a grade to a student by a teacher is regarded as antithetical to the self-concept of an adult. Therefore, self-assessment is encouraged with the teacher assisting students to collect evidence for themselves about their progress.

The procedures used in the diagnosis of learning needs are reapplied to assess gains in competence. This process also provides evaluation data and the teacher must be prepared to receive feedback on his own strengths and weaknesses.

2. *The student's experience.* Knowles argues that children have little experience which is of use to them as a resource in learning. Adults, however, have both a greater volume and different quality of experience because they have occupied many roles. This assumption has implications as follows:

(a) Experiential learning methods which tap the rich resource of experience which adults bring to any learning situation are the most appropriate methods. (For a fuller review of experiential learning see Miles, 1987.) Techniques for transmitting masses of information, such as the lecture method, should be minimized and greater emphasis placed on participatory learning.
(b) There should be an emphasis on the practical application of learning with opportunities for students to try out or rehearse new learning.
(c) Opportunities for 'unfreezing and learning to learn from experience' (Knowles, 1970) should be provided early in an educational programme. Adults may need to learn how to take responsibility for their own learning and how to learn collaboratively.

3. *Readiness to learn.* In children readiness to learn is largely a function of age. For example, Piaget outlines a number of developmental phases through which children pass during cognitive development. Tasks which require a certain order of thinking can not be learnt until a stage of cognitive development has been reached which enables thinking at this level. Table 3.1 outlines Piaget's stages of intellectual development.

Table 3.1 Piaget's stages of cognitive development

Stage	Age
Sensorimotor	0–2 years
Preoperational	2–7 years
Concrete operational	7–12 years
Formal operational	12 +

Adults, however, become ready to learn when they 'experience a need to know or do something in order to be able to perform more effectively in some aspect of their lives' (Knowles 1985). Knowles accepts that adults too have phases of growth, developmental tasks and 'teachable moments' but argues that these are essentially to do with the evolution of social roles. Cross (1981) has undertaken an extensive review of a range of developmental theories which focus on developmental tasks through adulthood and Knowles asserts that such phases are different from the physiological or mental maturational phases in early life. This assumption has implications as follows:

(a) Curriculum design should accommodate the adult's readiness to learn in terms of their real-life concerns and developmental tasks and not of the logic of the subject matter.
(b) Students should be grouped homogeneously where a common developmental task predominates as the learning need, and heterogeneously where learning would be enhanced by a cross-section of participants.

4. *Orientation to learning.* Children enter learning activities with a subject-centred orientation and see learning as a process of acquiring prescribed subject matter. Adults enter learning activities with a life-centred, task-centred problem orientation to learning. Children's learning tends to be for postponed application, whereas adults require immediacy of application. This belief has implications as follows:

(a) Adult educators should be student-centred in their approach and focus on the real-life concerns of students.
(b) The curriculum should address problem areas rather than specific subjects.
(c) The learning experience should be designed to achieve the expectations of students and commence with a period during which these expectations are explored and made explicit.

Knowles is not without his critics who have pointed out that many of his assumptions have not been sufficiently supported by research. Apps has, for example, argued that the so called unique approaches of adult educators are equally applicable to children and that 'children as learners are more like adults than they are different, granting differences such as those discussed by Piaget' (Apps, 1979).

There is little doubt that andragogy has had an impact on nurse education, although the basic premise on which andragogy is founded, the distinction between children and adults as learners, has been challenged (Elias, 1979) and debated vigorously (McKenzie, 1979). Knudson (1979) has proposed the term humanagogy as an all embracing concept of teaching and learning which takes account of the differences and similarities of people of all ages, but Jarvis (1983a) points out that such an inclusive concept is indistinct from what we currently regard as education.

There is now increasing evidence in nurse education of a general inclination towards andragogical approaches and in particular the use of 'contract-learning' in post-basic programmes (Whittaker, 1984; Keyzer, 1986; Akinsanya, 1987). This movement towards establishing a partnership between teacher and student is of particular relevance to clinical supervisors who are ideally placed to utilize facilitative skills (see Chapter Eight) to negotiate and respond to student needs.

But the approach is not without its limitations, and clinical supervisors, whether convinced by the basic andragogical premise or not, may find it difficult to focus on students' real-life concerns, as advocated by Knowles, within the confines of a structured curriculum as part of a statutory training (this tension between student-centred and institutional-centred education will be further explored later in this chapter). However, the andragogical view that curricula should be organized around problem areas rather than subjects or disciplines may appeal to clinical supervisors, who might legitimately assert that the predominantly topic-centred teaching in schools of nursing is poor preparation for clinical practice. Teaching in the clinical setting lends itself to a 'here and now' problem-centred approach.

Whether or not one takes issue with the assumptions that are made in andragogical theory, Knowles and others have been successful in ensuring that adult educators (not least nurse educationists) reflect on the implications of their students' maturity for the educational process. A summary of the andragogical paradigm is shown in Table 3.2, but it might also be useful to consider the features identified by Knowles as distinguishing children (and pedagogy) from

Table 3.2 The andragogical paradigm

1. Pre-active phase

   (a) Learning needs are identified by a process of self-diagnosis in which an amalgam of student and teacher expectations are defined as competencies. The student's present level of competence is assessed and the gap between this and the target level identified. The students' dissatisfaction is mobilized as a motivator to self improvement.
   (b) Planning the learning experience is a mutual activity between student and teacher, who acts a procedural guide and resource. Diagnosed needs are translated into specific educational objectives.

2. Interactive phase

   The teaching-learning transaction is a mutual responsibility with the teacher acting as a catalyst in facilitating student learning. Experiential methods predominate with the active participation of the student(s). Application of learning is emphasized and opportunities created for rehearsal.

3. Evaluative phase

   (a) Self assessment is advocated with the teacher assisting the student(s) to gather evidence about progress. The methods used to diagnose learning needs are reapplied.
   (b) This process also serves to provide evidence of the strengths and weaknesses of the teacher and the educational process.

adults (and andragogy) as a series of polar extremes in between which it is possible to plot the position of a given educational experience. This might be done proactively when planning the most appropriate approach to a given teacher-student encounter or retrospectively as an evaluation exercise (see Fig. 3.2). Clinical supervisors may wish to use the scale to plot their own ideological predisposition as both supervisors and as students. Discordant responses would serve well as a focus for discussion with colleagues about the assumptions we all have about the roles of teacher and student.

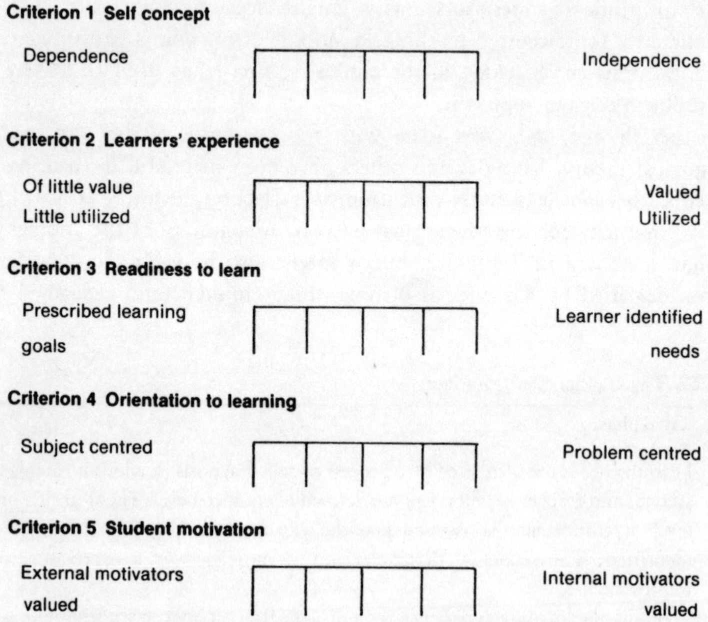

Criterion 1 Self concept

Dependence   Independence

Criterion 2 Learners' experience

Of little value   Valued
Little utilized   Utilized

Criterion 3 Readiness to learn

Prescribed learning   Learner identified
goals   needs

Criterion 4 Orientation to learning

Subject centred   Problem centred

Criterion 5 Student motivation

External motivators   Internal motivators
valued   valued

Fig. 3.2 Pedagogy-andragogy scale

Behavioural approaches

Behaviourists explain learning in terms of stimulus and response and consider that learning has taken place when a relatively permanent change in behaviour has occurred. The work of Pavlov (1894–1936) is frequently cited to illustrate the principles of 'classical conditioning' in which an unconditioned stimulus is paired with a conditioning stimulus for a period of time until the response to the unconditioned stimulus becomes associated with the conditioning stimulus. The same response can then be elicited by the conditioning stimulus alone. The conditioning of dogs to salivate (as in some of Pavlov's original experiments) is shown in Fig. 3.3 to illustrate this.

In the 1920s Watson demonstrated how it was possible to condition a child to

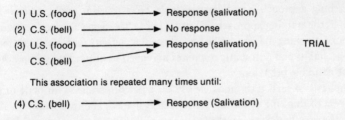

Fig. 3.3 Classical conditioning

fear an object. By creating a loud bang behind the child each time it reached to touch a white rat the child 'learnt' to fear the rat and soon became frightened merely at the sight of a rat. It has been suggested that adult phobias may also have their origins in (non-experimental) associative learning of this type in early life.

Elaboration of these fundamental principles of behavioural learning is evident in the work of Hull (1884–1952), who argued that there are variables which intervene between stimulus and response which either facilitate or inhibit the stimulus-response association. The work of Thorndike (1874–1949) has contributed to the further development of behavioural theory, in particular to the notion that much learning occurs through S-R associations derived from trial and error. Essentially, behaviour which results in success or reward is more likely to occur again than behaviour which does not. Thus, reward serves to strengthen a particular behaviour while the absence of reward weakens it.

Perhaps the most significant contribution to the behavioural psychology of learning was that of B. F. Skinner who developed the theory of 'operant conditioning'. Like other behaviourists, much of Skinner's work was carried out in laboratory settings on animals. In the now famous 'Skinner Box' exploratory activity by rats or other animals resulted in them pressing a bar accidentally, for which they were rewarded with food. After several such accidental behaviours Skinner observed that pressing the bar became an intentional behaviour. What originated as accidental behaviour became operant behaviour (that is, it operated on the environment) directed at achieving a reward. Further experimentation enabled Skinner to show that behaviour could be shaped by applying particular reinforcement (reward) contingencies. In successive experiments, Skinner was able to 'teach' a variety of animals relatively complex behavioural patterns (Skinner, 1951).

Operant conditioning is the basis for programmed learning, popular in the 1950s and 1960s, to which some readers may have been exposed during nurse training. Skinner (1968) has asserted that 'teaching is the arrangement of contingencies of reinforcement under which students learn'. Note that learning is construed as the acquisition of new behaviour through the manipulation of rewards and punishments. Many readers will be aware of the impact of this assumption on treatment strategies for the mentally handicapped and the mentally ill.

The teaching approach which derives from behaviourism might usefully be referred to as the training approach. Walton (1971) has suggested that 'according to this theory, teaching may be defined briefly as that activity which seeks to form associations, habits and automatic responses in oneself or others that will produce patterns of desirable behaviour'. '

The emphasis in such training is clearly on overt behaviour with little or no consideration of thinking or feeling. Behaviour is shaped, and thus learning takes place, by the manipulation of the environment in the form of rewards and punishments, although Skinner has argued that punishment should be avoided. The training approach is summarized in Table 3.3.

Behaviourism has had a significant impact on nurse training but three areas in particular are worthy of further consideration. These are rewards, behavioural objectives and skills learning. Central to the behavioural or training approach is the significance of reinforcement or rewards for desired behaviours. While rewards such as tokens or stars and activities such as games, may have a role in the education of young children, adults are more likely to respond to social rewards such as praise or recognition, or to internal rewards related to self-esteem and

---

Table 3.3   The training paradigm

1. Pre-active phase

(a) Learning needs are assessed against the required behaviour specified by the employer or training institution.

(b) Planning involves an analysis of the task to be learnt and the explicit specification of terminal behavioural objectives. The task may be broken down into knowledge content and skill content. Effective reinforcers (motivators) are identified for students.

2. Interactive phase

The student's 'entry' behaviour is observed and then by means of teacher demonstration or verbal instruction the teacher elicits student responses which constitute steps on the way from initial or 'entry' behaviour to terminal behaviour. Performances which approximate to the specified terminal behavioural objectives are immediately reinforced while the requirements for gaining reward are successively increased until the complete behavioural performance is exhibited.

3. Evaluative phase

Assessment is simply the process of establishing whether the students have achieved the desired terminal behaviour. If not, the teaching continues until such time as they do, possibly by increasing the number of steps thus increasing the likelihood of success and reinforcement.

Finally, it is assumed that the learned behaviour can be transferred from simulated conditions to the real situation. Reinforcement of success in the 'real world' may further strengthen the behaviour.

---

self-concept. Having said this, any reader who has been successful in the simplest of computer games will attest to the reward value of the most banal jingle in reinforcing the behaviour.

The important point is that whilst few nurse educators would subscribe to a purist behavioural model most recognize the importance of rewards in reinforcing learning. On the basis that rewarded behaviour tends to be repeated it is a productive teaching technique. Clinical supervisors should be ready to give immediate feedback to learners practising clinical skills but especially when students can be congratulated for mastering new or complex procedures. Since adult learning is probably far more complex than the behavioural model allows, immediate concrete feedback may not be the only or most effective form of reinforcement.

Self-esteem and a sense of success or achievement seem to be potent motivators to learning. Clinical supervisors may find that students respond best to limited criticism with periodic praise for their work in general. A 'well done' from the charge nurse at the end of the shift in recognition for the successful completion of a range of duties may serve as a more efficient reinforcer than more immediate tangible rewards.

Although the influence of behaviourism is receding and concerns have been expressed regarding the value of objectives in nurse education (Gibson, 1980), the impact of behavioural objectives on nurse education should not be underestimated. Behavioural objectives in curriculum design are discussed further in Chapter Four but a comprehensive review can be found in Davies (1976). Despite considerable debate in educational circles about the merits of behavioural objectives most nurse teachers have found them of value. In particular it has been suggested that they serve three broad purposes (Davies, 1976):

1. They serve as guides to teaching and curriculum planning.
2. They serve as guides to learning.
3. They serve as guides to teacher and learner evaluation.

In reviewing empirical evidence Davies goes on to suggest that what research has been done implies that:

1. General objectives are as effective as specific objectives.
2. Action verbs are the most critical part of the objectives.
3. Training teachers in the use of objectives as guides to teaching is worthwhile.
4. Children (and one has to decide whether the research can be extrapolated to adults) taught by teachers using objectives learn more than children taught by teachers not using objectives.

It would seem that the discipline of stating outcome objectives explicitly when designing a learning or teaching programme is worth the sometimes protracted planning. Clinical supervisors may already be aware of this truism from experience in setting objectives in patient care plans.

Finally, another area where behaviourism and the training approach has been of value is in skills learning. Much of nursing practice requires technical competence and clinical supervisors will frequently be involved in teaching psychomotor skills. The mechanistic approach of behaviourism and the emphasis on overt behaviour makes it an admirable model from which to plan skills teaching. Stones (1979) provides a useful checklist for teachers which he refers to as STOPS (schedule for the teaching of psychomotor skills). What follows in Table 3.4 is an abridged and adapted version appropriate for use by clinical supervisors in nurse education.

The behavioural or training approach has many critics and few nurse educators

Table 3.4 Skills teaching schedule

Pre-active phase

1. Undertake a task analysis of the skill or teaching objectives. Decide the following.
   (a) Methods of presentation.
   (b) The nature of student activities.
   (c) The provision of feedback.
   (d) Evaluation of performance.
   (e) The arrangements for monitored practice.

2. Assess the students' existing level of competence. Students lacking the prerequisite motor abilities may require remedial teaching. (Readers might like to recall the first occasion they attempted to attach a needle and syringe, and draw up solution from a sealed bottle!).

Interactive phase

3. .Explain and demonstrate the task.
4. Idenfity the component skills and demonstrate their relationship to the whole task.
5. Encourage the student to describe the activity, possibly by guiding the teacher in performing the task.
6. Prompt and guide the student in carrying out the component skills involved in the task.
7. Prompt and guide the student in making a smooth transition from one component to another.
8. Reduce the prompts and guidance to encourage the student to assume responsibility.
9. Provide feedback at all stages and reward all appropriate responses.
10. Arrange for practice to encourage the student to consolidate the skill.
11. Monitor the practice intermittently.
12. Encourage application in varying circumstances.

Evaluative phase

13. Assess the level of success of the student's performance against the objectives.
14. Encourage the student to assess his own practice against criteria established in the interactive phase (3, 4, 5).

espouse a purist application of behavioural principles. But the general acceptance of the importance of rewards as reinforcement of learning, of behavioural objectives as signposts for learning and of a structured and systematic approach to skills teaching ensures the continued utility of behavioural theories in nurse education.

The humanistic approach

The humanistic approach to education can be seen as a rebuttal of the behavioural approach which emphasizes the impact of environmental reinforcers in 'shaping' behaviour. Humanistic psychologists such as Abraham Maslow and Carl Rogers emphasize the control an individual has over his environment and his learning. They believe that individuals have an innate potential for growth and development and that teachers should be concerned with facilitating this natural process.

This approach to teaching derives particularly from the work of Carl Rogers, who has written extensively in the field of counselling and psychotherapy. The approach Rogers advocates is often referred to as non-directive counselling, and focuses on the human qualities of the counsellor in conveying warmth and empathy to the client, who, through the expression of these counsellor qualities is encouraged towards a greater understanding of self and others and to a resolution of problems. The focus is phenomenological in the sense that the counsellor does not impose a frame of reference or interpretation on the client's experience but rather facilitates exploration of how the client sees and experiences the world.

These assumptions about how best humans can be encouraged to develop have been transferred to the field of education. Since both counselling and teaching are regarded as helping activities, the assumptions about an innate motivation towards self-actualization (Maslow, 1970) and the importance of empathic qualities in counsellors apply equally to teacher–learner transactions.

In the now seminal work *Freedom to Learn*, Rogers (1969) identifies what might be regarded as the key features of the humanistic approach to education. These can be summarized as follows:

1. Individuals have a natural drive to learn, particularly if that learning is perceived by the individual as maintaining or enhancing his self-concept.
2. Learning is best achieved in these conditions.
   (a) In a trusting, non-threatening climate.
   (b) Through experience.
   (c) When there is mutual participation of student and teacher in setting aims, organizing content, identifying resources and accepting the consequences of choices of action.
   (d) When it involves feelings and intellect.
   (e) When self-evaluation is encouraged, facilitating independence, creativity and self-reliance.

Rogers (1969) also presents some guidelines for facilitators of learning which are in essence as follows.

1. The facilitator is first concerned with establishing a climate of trust.
2. The facilitator seeks clarification of the students' aims and tolerates a diversity of goals within a group.
3. The facilitator relies on the motivation of each student to pursue his own aims, which are significant only to him.
4. The facilitator makes available, or ensures access, to the widest range of resources for learning.
5. The facilitator acts in a flexible way as a resource to the group.
6. The facilitator recognizes and accepts both students' thoughts and feelings, giving due weight to each.
7. The facilitator becomes a participant student as the group develops.
8. The facilitator shares his own thoughts and feelings with the group.
9. The facilitator is alert to tensions and conflicts in the group which are utilized as learning resources.
10. The facilitator is aware of and accepts his strengths and weaknesses as a facilitator and as a resource.

Unlike the behavioural approach discussed earlier in this chapter, the Rogerian perspective is not really based on empirical research although Rogers cites persuasive case examples in his writings. Regardless of the empirical validity of this model, Rogers has been successful in drawing attention to the importance of the personal relationship between teacher and student (Brophy and Good, 1974).

The humanistic or non-directive approach to teaching is outlined in summary form in Table 3.5.

Table 3.5 The humanistic paradigm

1. Pre-active phase

(a) Learning needs are identified through a shared analysis of the student's phenomen-ological field (personal experience).
(b) The process of planning is a joint venture in which the student and facilitator evolve objectives of a general nature and through empathic interaction.

2. Interactive phase

Note that the framework for summarizing teaching approaches used falls down here because interaction is not simply the instructional phase but is the focus of mutual exploration throughout the whole teaching-learning cycle in this paradigm. However, instruction, such as it is, involves interaction of an exploratory open-ended nature, in particular, the facilitation of experiential learning.

3. Evaluative phase

The encounter is evaluated in terms of changes in self-concept, self-determination, relationships with others and achievement of self-actualization.

The non-directive humanistic approach has received considerable attention from nurse teachers in recent years, in particular those in psychiatric nursing who value the personal growth in students which emanates from learner-centred teaching. The use of experiential learning strategies, now commonplace in many nursing curricula, owes much to the learner-centred orientation asserted by Rogers.

This approach is of direct relevance to clinical supervisors who are ideally placed to facilitate learning through and from experience. An experiential learning cycle is shown as Fig. 3.4 in which it can be seen that the supervisor has a key role in facilitating the process of learning.

The clinical supervisor is clearly in a position to exert some control over the quantity and quality of experience(s) available to the student (A). Equally by utilizing the facilitative skills identified by Rogers he can facilitate learning through an exploration and analysis of that experience (B and C), the formulation of new or enhanced understandings and proposals for modifying future actions (D). This facilitative process need not be time consuming. Whilst it might take the form of a formal supervisory tutorial, it might also simply occur as encouragement to a student to consider some recent aspect of practice during a few moments while continuing to work together on the ward.

Although schools of nursing are concerned to equip students with the necessary knowledge and skills to function effectively in the clinical setting, theory does not always precede practice. Since much of a nurse's education is spent in the clinical field it seems entirely appropriate that measures are taken to enhance learning through and from experience. There is room both for learning which involves theory followed by practice and practice followed by theory; indeed both processes may be necessary properly to ensure nursing competence.

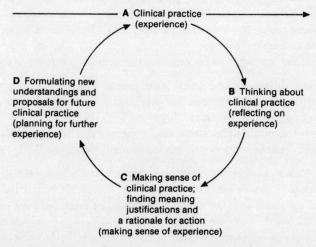

Fig. 3.4 An experiential learning cycle

Cognitive approaches

Unlike behaviourists, cognitive psychologists place emphasis on the way in which the brain processes information and the influence cognitive structures acquired from experience have on the organization and acquisition of knowledge. The Gestalt school (Wertheimer, Kohler, Koffka *et al.*), working on perception as means of understanding learning, asserted that man tends to perceive things in wholes rather than as the components which make up the whole. From experimental evidence the Gestalt school argued that a learner's perception of a problem undergoes a restructuring so that the elements of the problem are perceived in a new relationship to one another, thus enabling a solution by 'insight'. It was demonstrated that animals solved problems after a period of appraisal and apparent puzzlement. No reinforcement to 'shape' behaviour as indicated by the behaviourists was apparent.

Other theorists have developed more complex explanations of cognitive learning. David Ausubel (1968) argues that learning takes place as a result of interaction between new information which the learner is acquiring and his existing cognitive structures. Assimilation of the new material through an interaction of old and new results in the formulation of a new more detailed cognitive structure. A key feature of Ausubel's theory is this linking of new to old which he refers to as meaningful learning. He distinguishes this from rote learning by suggesting that the former can be applied critically in novel situations, whereas the latter can not. He further argues that rote learning is more likely to be forgotten. For Ausubel, meaningful learning is not a passive process. The student has actively to engage in a process of 'judging which concept or proposition to catalogue the new knowledge under' (Joyce and Weil, 1972).

His detailed elaboration of this point supports the view that so-called passive expository teaching (i.e. the lecture method) does not necessarily lead to rote learning. The determining factor is how the teaching is conducted, and on this basis Ausubel's theory has a number of implications for teachers regarding the organization of learning material.

Two principles are suggested for programming content. These are as follows.

1. Progressive differentiation, which is the process whereby the 'most general ideas of the discipline or topic are presented first, followed by a gradual increase in detail and specificity' (Joyce and Weil, 1972).
2. Integrative reconciliation, which simply means 'that new ideas should be consciously related to previously learned content' (Joyce and Weil, 1972).

The curriculum is, therefore, structured in such a way that each successive learning task is related to what has gone before. This might be referred to as a 'top down' approach with an emphasis first on the most inclusive concepts, principles and propositions. An example is shown in Table 3.6 to illustrate how progressive differentiation might apply in the teaching of a new subject, in this instance 'nursing ethics'. Subsequent teaching would seek to establish links between this and new learning (integrative reconciliation).

Table 3.6 Progressive differentiation

Chronology of presentation		
1.	Topic area:	Nursing ethics
2.	Theories:	E.g. deontological (duty) based theories
3.	Ethical principles:	E.g. autonomy or respect for persons
4.	Ethical rules	E.g. 'act always in such a way as to respect the patient's right to self-determination'
5.	Actions:	E.g. the seeking of consent from a patient before proceeding with a nursing procedure

Ausubel also argues that learning is more effective if teachers establish what he refers to as advance organizers. Advance organizers are ideas of a very general and inclusive nature which provide an overview to the topic or material to be learned.

They are presented in advance of the new material and serve as a link between what the student already knows and the subsequent specific detail of what is to be learned. Whereas written objectives may be available to students in a school of nursing, clinical supervisors may wish to make verbally explicit any objectives at the outset of a supervisory session with students to serve as advance organizers. Alternatively, a midwifery clinical supervisor might explain briefly the concept of genetic abnormality (a general class or category) before discussing a specific example in the work that student midwives had encountered. The advance organizer serves to set the scene for the subsequent detailed information by distinguishing it as a class of things, as distinct, say, from trauma or infection. Other cognitive psychologists have favoured less directive methods than Ausubel.

Bruner for example is credited with having coined the term 'discovery learning'. Discovery learning occurs when a student is able to consider particular instances and from them devise a general case (induction), or by trial and error arrive at an acceptable generalization (errorful learning). It has been asserted that induction not only achieves an accumulation of knowledge but also equips students with problem-solving skills of value in other learning (Bruner, 1961).

Critics have, however, argued that where trial and error learning predominates there is a high probability of errors and mistakes and that the motivational advantages of discovery learning over rote learning are outweighed by the disadvantages of trial and error. In nurse education the acquisition of problem-solving skills is highly valued and discovery learning frequently advocated. While this may be appropriate in classroom simulations trial and error learning is not a method of choice in patient care areas for obvious reasons.

More recently cognitive psychologists have concentrated their efforts in devising computer models as analogies of human learning. Information-processing theories focus on systems of information encoding, retention and retrieval and highlight the importance of limiting the amount of information to be learned to prevent overload and also of the significance of feedback for students on their progress.

A number of implications arise from the cognitive perspective on teaching and learning. The emphasis in cognitive theories is on the accurate and efficient transmission of information, the assumption being that there exists a body of knowledge external to the student which he can acquire if the teacher is a sufficiently skilled communicator. The process of knowledge acquisition involves the reformulation of cognitive structures, or mental maps, in such a way as to accommodate and assimilate the new information. The method which predominates in this communication approach is the lecture, but this has been criticized as an ineffective teaching strategy. Bligh (1971) however, identifies a range of techniques which enhance the effectiveness of the lecture method, taking account of psychological and educational research.

A further communication approach which serves as the bedrock of all education and learning is, of course, the written word. This book is an example of the way in which material, new to some readers, has been organized and presented in a structure thought to be most effective in encouraging and assisting learning. Readers might like to consider whether the structure and sequence in this chapter has facilitated or inhibited learning. The assumptions and teaching implications of the cognitive or communication approach are detailed in Table 3.7.

One of a number of approaches to teaching and learning which does not fit neatly into the categorization used here is that of social learning theory and the work of Albert Bandura. This is an important additional theory to draw

Table 3.7 The cognitive paradigm

---

1. Pre-active phase

    (a) Learning needs are considered to be the difference between what students know and what an external authority (e.g. English National Board, School of Nursing or clinical supervisor) believes they ought to know derived from an analysis of the discipline (nursing).

    (b) Decisions are made about the most effective ways of organizing and presenting new material.

2. Interactive phase

The emphasis is on structured, highly organized presentations, usually in the form of lectures or the written word together with audio-visual aids. Information is organized hierarchically or sequentially and presented in a clear concise form.

3. Evaluative phase

The outcome is measured in terms of the degree to which new knowledge has been acquired. This is often measured by formal examination, usually in the form of unseen questions or objective tests.

---

attention to because it goes some way to explaining what many clinical supervisors would regard as an important aspect of their role, that of functioning as a role model.

Social learning theorists argue that much learning is acquired by observation of role models. It is possible that student nurses acquire much of their 'professional' behaviour by a process of identification with role models (skilled practitioners) and imitate this behaviour until, through a process of internalization, it becomes part and parcel of their own behavioural repertoire.

Bandura (1973) cites convincing evidence of the impact of models on the development of aggressive behaviour in children. If such 'modelling' is as pervasive as some theorists assert, then clinical supervisors are constantly in a position of being 'on show' as exemplars of their art. This theory of course also accounts, to some extent, for the many 'short-cuts' that nursing students acquire in their practice which nobody will admit to having taught them!

NURSES FOR THE 1990S AND BEYOND

Against a background of demographic and economic changes and an increase in demand for health care, the United Kingdom Central Council for Nursing, Midwifery and Health Visiting has published proposals for radical revison in the way in which nurses are prepared for clinical practice (UKCC, 1986). Conceptions of what knowledge, skills and values nurses require influence the type of teaching-learning strategies adopted. Clinical supervisors will be particularly concerned with how best they can assist in the development of 'knowledgeable doers' (UKCC, 1986). Before exploring this goal in more detail it is perhaps worth setting it in context.

The general public quite rightly expect nurses to be competent to care for them and invest responsibility for this in the statutory bodies, who, through act of parliament, are charged with the creation and maintenance of professional nursing standards. This is achieved in the United Kingdom through the maintenance of a single professional register of nurses licensed to practise, a code of professional conduct (UKCC, 1984) and machinery to ensure professional discipline and the validation of basic and post-basic trainings (the latter function delegated in the United Kingdom to four National Boards). These statutory structures are important to all those involved in nurse education because they dictate to a certain extent choices of educational strategy.

This is evident in a tension discussed earlier in this chapter between the institutional or statutory demands of a professionally validated training (for example the competencies defined in Statutory Instrument 873 (1983) or the EC directives on clinical experience) and some educational approaches (for example the liberal regime of the humanistic approach). This kind of tension has been ably demonstrated by Jarvis (1986) who identifies two curricula models to show the differing assumptions and demands of competing models of the educational process. He refers to one as 'education from above' and to the other as the 'education of equals'. This distinction is not dissimilar to Knowles's perception of pedagogy and andragogy.

Education from above involves a teacher- or institution-centred approach with decisions regarding aims, objectives, content, methods and assessment and evaluation being made for the students by the teacher or institution. Conversely, the education of equals is student-centred with teachers fulfilling a facilitative role in negotiating needs, goals, content, methods, assessment and evaluation with the student(s). The appropriateness of either model is dependent on which of two assumptions about socialization (and education as an important aspect of it) one espouses. If one believes that individuals are the product of the social systems in which they are located, then the most effective educational approach will be education from above. If, however, one believes that social systems are the product of the individuals who comprise them, then the education of equals model is the most appropriate form of socialization.

Jarvis goes on to make explicit the importance of this line of reasoning. He asks, 'does nursing require practitioners who are compliant to the demands from above or ones who are able to be self-directing?' (Jarvis, 1986). The answer to this question will determine which is the most appropriate approach. Two conceptions of the ideal nurse (perhaps past and present) can be compared to demonstrate the link between such conceptions and educational models. (See Fig. 3.5).

Assuming that readers will agree that we are concerned today with facilitating the development of Type B nurses for the 1990s, and that such a goal is best

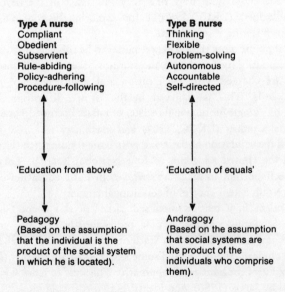

Fig. 3.5 Two conceptions of the ideal nurse

served by an 'education of equals' approach our next task is to identify teaching strategies likely to succeed. Given the statutory requirements and institutional constraints outlined earlier the need is for an approach which draws both from the andragogical and humanistic paradigms as well as the behavioural and cognitive paradigms more commonly associated with the pedagogical approach.

Clinical supervisors and all nurse educationists will need to establish an eclectic model informed by the strengths of all four paradigms addressed earlier in this chapter if the goal is to produce a 'knowledgeable doer' (UKCC, 1986). The general public legitimately claim not only technical competence but also interpersonal sensitivity and moral integrity of qualified nurses. Nurse education will only achieve these goals if nurse educators are both bold enough to tolerate, analyse and synthesize knowledge from a variety of sometimes competing educational perspectives to inform and support their teaching practice.

Monistic or extremist positions have no place in a professional education aimed at developing nursing practitioners for the 1990s and beyond. Only through the development of an eclectic model will the tensions between statutory requirements and educational dogma be resolved.

The 'knowledgeable doer' – a strategy for action

Davies has identified three value systems which underpin approaches to curriculum design and teaching strategies. These demonstrate how a modern perspective is 'an amalgam of what is hopefully best and appropriate' drawn from the classical and romantic perspectives of the educational process (Davies, 1976). (See Table 3.8.)

Table 3.8 Three perspectives

Classical perspective	Romantic perspective	Modern perspective
Autocratic	Laissez-faire	Participative
Conservative	Abdication	Liberal
Subject emphasis	Method emphasis	Process emphasis
Teacher-centred	Student-centred	Inquiry-centred
Active	Reactive	Transactive
Creativity	Confusion	Probability
Discipline	Freedom	Responsibility
Doing things to	Doing things for	Doing things with

(Adapted from Davies, 1976)

In seeking justification for teaching practices, clinical supervisors might usefully consider which aspects of the four paradigms discussed best support an approach which is in keeping with the values Davies (1976) has described in the 'modern perspective'. Consideration will now be given to a teaching strategy, described in the three phases used throughout this chapter (see Fig. 3.6) which seeks to provide eclectic and pragmatic guidance for clinical supervisors.

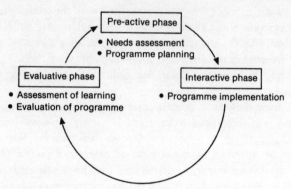

Fig. 3.6 The teaching cycle

Pre-active phase

There are two principal elements to the pre-active phase: needs assessment and programme planning.

Bradshaw (1977) identifies four types of need; normative, felt, expressed and comparative. Normative needs are those which are defined by experts or professionals. Felt need are those which individuals experience for themselves and comparative needs are those which emerge when an individual compares himself to another. Expressed needs are those that amount to a demand for a response to satisfy a specified need. Figure 3.7 details the different forms of need to which the clinical supervisor may be exposed and required to mediate.

Drawing on the four paradigms discussed, learning needs should be the result of a negotiation process between supervisor and student, taking account of normative needs in the form of statutory competencies or National Board requirements, an assessment of present student competence by the supervisor (sometimes referred to as diagnostic appraisal), and the students' expressed felt and comparative needs. This process of negotiation and all subsequent teaching interactions require a high level of inter-personal skill. In reviewing the work of Rogers, Baath (1979) succinctly identifies the characteristics of a skilled facilitator of learning as follows.

1. Realness or genuineness.
2. Positive valuing of others.
3. Empathy.

If these qualities are present then the negotiation of learning needs will be a mutually satisfying and successful process for both student and supervisor and a climate of trust will have been established as the Rogerian approach demands.

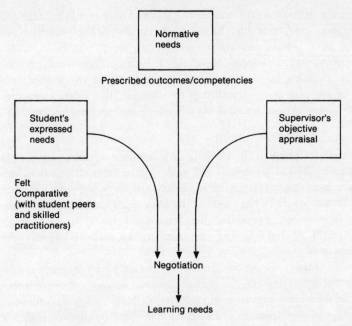

Fig. 3.7 Learning needs

Planning a teaching programme involves making decisions about the most appropriate content and method(s) to employ to achieve the agreed goals. The agreed goals which emerge from the needs assessment should be formulated into learning objectives to give both a focus and a structure to the learning experience. Whether these are in the form of behavioural objectives or not seems less important than is often thought, as discussed earlier in this chapter (see Davies, 1976). Insights drawn from the cognitive paradigm will assist clinical supervisors in selecting, structuring and sequencing the content of teaching sessions but it should be acknowledged that much of a clinical supervisor's teaching role involves facilitating experiential learning which does not require the isolation of detailed knowledge in advance.

Clinical supervisors will more frequently be confronted with student-generated or facilitated material with which the student requires assistance to structure during phases of the experiential learning cycle.

A wide variety of teaching methods is available to the teacher to achieve differing objectives, but in clinical practice supervisors are less likely to make a firm decision in advance as to whether to lecture, or to lead a discussion, for example, than they are to adopt various roles in the facilitation of learning. This latter approach is taken up in the next section, the interactive phase.

Planning a learning experience or teaching activity involves ensuring that all resources are available when required. This may require negotiation with other staff to establish that the students are free at a given time, or it may require booking a quiet room on the ward or unit and making sure that any teaching aids are prepared and available. Ensuring the availability of teaching-learning resources is a vitally important function which, if not effected, detracts significantly from any learning experience. It is also perhaps worth pointing out here that planning learning experiences not only relates to specified times or activities but also involves ensuring, for example, that reference sources and relevant journal articles are available to students during clinical placements.

Interactive phase

The interactive phase of the teaching cycle involves implementing the planned programme. Clinical supervisors will wish to draw from all four paradigms for guidance, but in particular the andragogical emphasis on respecting the student as an adult and equal in the inquiry, the humanistic paradigm with regard to facilitator qualities and skills, the behavioural model as a rationale for reinforcement of learning and the cognitive approach as regards effective communication.

As highlighted in the previous section the clinical supervisor's role is primarily facilitative and is unlikely to involve frequent decisions about whether, for example, the lecture method or guided study is the most appropriate method to achieve given objectives. In order to provide some framework within which clinical supervisors can operate Heron's *Dimensions of Facilitator Style* is suggested (Heron, 1977). This model is a development of, and complements *Six Category Intervention Analysis* (Heron, 1975) which is used in Chapter Eight in a more extensive review of facilitation skills. Heron identifies six dimensions which are here adapted to the teaching situation and detailed together with the intervention each relates to in the Six Category Intervention Model:

1. Directive–non-directive dimension. Here the teacher either takes responsibility for the teaching-learning experience or delegates it to the student or group (this corresponds to the prescriptive category).
2. Interpretative–non-interpetative dimension. Here the teacher either conceptualizes and gives meaning to what is occurring in the learning experience to the student(s) or leaves this to the student or group (this corresponds with the informative category).
3. Confronting–non-confronting dimension. Here the teacher either challenges (supportively) distorted or inaccurate thinking or creates a climate in which the student or group do this for themselves (this corresponds with the confronting category).
4. Cathartic–non-cathartic dimension. Here the teacher either encourages cathartic release in the student or group or creates a climate of tension-reduction without catharsis (this corresponds with the cathartic intervention).
   (Clinical supervisors may doubt the usefulness of this dimension but for those working in the psychiatric setting, or when dealing predominantly with attitudes or difficult situations such as death and dying, it is particularly important).

5. Structuring–unstructuring dimension. Here the teacher structures the learning process in order to control and provide a particular sequence to learning or encourages experiential learning that is consequent on no such structuring (this corresponds with the catalytic category).

6. Disclosing–non-disclosing dimension. Here the teacher either shares his own thoughts and feeling about the learning experience with the student or group or does not do so. (This corresponds with the supportive category.)

Using this model, and with reference to facilitative skills elaborated in Chapter Eight, clinical supervisors are in a position to judge where on the continuum for each dimension it is appropriate to be in a given teaching-learning transaction. Depending on the student(s) and the nature of the learning experience some situations demand a highly directive, structured, non-cathartic approach with little self-disclosure on the part of the supervisor. On the other hand, discussing the significance of the death of a longstanding patient, for example, may dictate a more non-directive, unstructured approach with the supervisor sharing in the process much more through self-disclosure and catharsis.

The teaching of technical skills may require a more structured and controlled approach such as that described in the section on behavioural approaches. The key functions of the supervisor in implementing a skills learning programme are to provide instruction, practice and feedback. But even this process can be illuminated by analysis using the six dimensions outlined above. Readers may wish to consider where on each dimension they should seek to function in order to provide effective instruction, practice and feedback. Such an analysis will highlight the need for successful facilitators of learning to be fluent in adopting different styles at appropriate points in the learning process.

Evaluative phase
There are two principal elements to this phase of the teaching-learning cycle. Firstly, the need to establish a measure of how much progress the student has made. Assessment of learning is dealt with fully in Chapter Nine and is not therefore explored further here.

The second element is evaluation of the learning experience in its entirety. It is not unusual for assessment and evaluation to be discordant, with students achieving learning goals not because of a teaching-learning programme but rather in spite of it. For this reason it is argued here that despite the implication of paradigms such as the behavioural approach it is important not only to assess student progress but also to evaluate the whole enterprise. There is, after all, no reason to assume that because student X has succeeded (perhaps in spite of a poor teaching programme) that subsequent students will too. The need for remedial action will only emerge from a full evaluation. This element too is dealt with more fully in Chapter Six.

CONCLUSION

This chapter has been concerned with defining teaching, learning and education and in elaborating four approaches which elucidate these processes. The implications of these approaches to nurse education have been highlighted and attention has been drawn to their contribution towards an eclectic approach to the preparation of nurses for the 1990s and beyond. The chapter has been concerned not only with educational theory but also with the practicalities faced by clinical supervisors in seeking theoretical support for their teaching practice. In conclusion, it is anticipated that the chapter will have provided a broad perspective on the education of adults sufficient to stimulate clinical supervisors to work actively in the preparation of 'knowledgeable doers' (UKCC, 1986).

REFERENCES

Akinsanya, J. (1987). 'Teaching by contract', *Senior Nurse* 7 (6): 26–7.

Apps, J. W. (1979). *Problems in Continuing Education*. New York: McGraw Hill.

Ausubel, D. (1968). *Educational Psychology: A Cognitive View*. New York: Holt, Rinehart and Winston.

Baath, J. A. (1979). *Correspondence Education in the Light of a Number of Contemporary Teaching Models*. Malino: Liber Hermods.

Bandura, A. (1973). *Aggression: A Social Learning Analysis*. Englewood Cliffs: Prentice Hall Inc.

Bligh, D. A. (1971). *What's the Use of Lectures?*. Exeter: D. A. and B. Bligh.

Bradshaw, J. (1977). Cited in Fitzgerald, M. *et al.* (eds), *Welfare in Action*. London: Routledge and Kegan Paul/Open University Press.

Brophy, J. E. and Good, T. L. (1974). *Teacher–Student Relationships*. New York: Holt, Rinehart and Winston.

Brunner (1961). 'The art of discovery', *Harvard Educational Review* 31: 21–32.

Cross, K. P. (1981). *Adults as Learners: Increasing Facilitation and Facilitating Learning*. San Francisco: Jossey Bass.

Davies, I. K. (1976). *Objectives in Curriculum Design*. London: McGraw Hill.

Elias, J. L. (1979). 'Andragogy revisited', *Adult Education* 29: 252–6.

Gibson, S. (1980). 'A critique of the objectives model in curriculum design', *Journal of Advanced Nursing* 5 (2): 161–7.

Heron, J. (1975). *Six Category Intervention Analysis*. Surrey University: Human Potential Research Project.

Heron, J. (1977). *Dimensions of Facilitator Style*. London: British Postgraduate Medical Association.

Hilgard, E. R. *et al.* (1975). *Introduction to Psychology*, 6th edn. New York: Harcourt Brace Jovanovich.

Jarvis, P. (1983a). *Adult and Continuing Education: Theory and Practice*. Beckenham: Croom Helm.

Jarvis, P. (1983b). *Professional Education*. Beckenham: Croom Helm.

Jarvis, P. (1986). 'Nurse education and adult education: a question of the person'. *Journal of Advanced Nursing* (11): 465–9.

Joyce, B. and Weil, M. (1972). *Models of Teaching*. Englewood Cliffs: Prentice Hall Inc.

Keyzer, D. (1986). 'Using learning contracts to support change in nursing organisations',

Nurse Education Today 6: 103–8.

Knowles, M. (1970). *The Modern Practice of Adult Education: Andragogy versus Pedagogy.* Chicago: Follett.

Knowles, M. and Associates (1985). *Andragogy in Action: Applying Modern Principles of Adult Education.* San Francisco: Jossey Bass.

Knudson, R. S. (1979). 'Humanagogy anyone', *Adult Education* 29: 216–64.

McKenzie, L. (1979). 'A response to Elias', *Adult Education* 29: 256–61.

Maslow, A. (1970). *Motivation and Personality,* 2nd edn. New York: Harper and Row.

Miles, R. (1987). 'Experiential learning in the curriculum' in P. Allen and M. Jolly (eds), *The Curriculum in Nursing Education.* Beckenham: Croom Helm.

Moore, M. (1984). *Concepts of Adult Education* (E335, Block A). Milton Keynes: Open University Press.

Rogers, C. (1969). *Freedom to Learn.* Ohio: Merril.

Skinner, B. F. (1951). 'How to teach animals', *Scientific American,* December 1951.

Skinner, B. F. (1968). *The Technology of Teaching.* New York: Appleton-Century-Croft.

Stones, E. (1979). *Psychopedagogy.* London: Methuen.

Statutory Instrument 873 (1983). *The Nurses, Midwives and Health Visitor's Rules, Approval Order.* London: HMSO.

Tough, A. (1971). *The Adult's Learning Projects: A Fresh Approach to Theory and Practice in Adult Learning.* Toronto: Ontario Institute for Studies in Education, Research in Education, Series No 1.

United Kingdom Central Council for Nursing, Midwifery and Health Visiting (1986). *Project 2000.* London: UKCC.

United Kingdom Central Coucil for Nursing, Midwifery and Health Visiting (1984). *Code of Professional Conduct for the Nurse, Midwife and Health Visitor,* 2nd ed. London: UKCC.

Walton, J. (1971). 'Four theories of teaching' in R. Hyman (ed.), *Contemporary thought on teaching.* Englewood Cliffs: Prentice Hall Inc.

Whittaker, A. F. (1984). 'Use of contract learning', *Nurse Education Today* 4 (2): 36–40.

CHAPTER FOUR

THE DEVELOPMENT OF NURSING CURRICULA

INTRODUCTION

Selecting a career is one of the most important choices an individual makes. Entrants to nursing may make their decisions on the knowledge they have gained previously, perhaps through actual experience as a patient or through relatives or friends who have been patients. Alternatively knowledge may be gained through literature, television documentaries and other programmes, and some may have held jobs as care assistants or auxiliary nurses. When training commences each student has some idea of what will be achieved and assessed. Thus each entrant to nursing has a personal idea of the contents of the nursing curriculum. Practising nurses also have views of the nursing curriculum based on past learning experiences and current involvement with their patients and with students in training. Nurse educationalists also have perceptions of the nursing curriculum based on the philosophy and practices of the School of Nursing and their personal experiences of curriculum design. Conflict may occur if the various perspectives of these groups differ. It is therefore of value for practising nurses to have an understanding of curriculum design and the factors that influence it in order to contribute effectively to implementation, evaluation and development of the curriculum.

DEFINING THE CURRICULUM

The term curriculum is sometimes confused with other educational terms such as syllabus, timetable and allocation programme. These are all different aspects of education and may be defined as follows.

The Syllabus is a list of subject matter for a course of study: the timetable lists the specific lessons, their venues and the teachers involved: the allocation programme plans learning experiences, both theoretical and clinical, spanning the course of training. There are many definitions of the word curriculum but perhaps one that is relevent to nursing is that by Kerr (1968) as cited in Quinn (1980).

Curriculum: All the learning which is planned and guided by the school, whether it is carried out in groups or individually, inside or outside the school.

This definition suggests three major points, firstly that learning is planned and guided by the school. In a generalized sense this is correct for it is possible to plan theoretical sessions and practical experiences in the required elements for the particular field of nursing. However it may be impossible to plan all the specific learning experiences. For example, whilst it may be desirable for all students to deal in practice with a cardiac arrest, this experience cannot be guaranteed and some may only learn in theory how to deal with this situation.

The second point is that learning may be carried on in groups or individually. The nature of nurse training is such that students are likely to learn in groups in both the classroom and clinical areas and will also spend time working individually both academically and in nursing practice. In traditional training courses the large proportion of time spent in the clinical environment makes it necessary to provide a positive learning climate where maximum use is made of learning opportunities and that these are related to the individual learning needs of the student. Theoretical learning continues throughout clinical placements, partly by tutorials within the clinical area, partly by interblock personal study and partly by work set by the school. This learning is likely to take place both in groups and individually.

Thirdly, the definition suggests that learning may be carried on inside or outside the school. It may be suggested that in nursing the school is anywhere the student is, not just the physical building that is labelled the School of Nursing. However, the students will also learn from aspects of their life which may be defined as being 'outside the school'. Life experiences are also learning experiences and contribute to the knowledge, skills and attitudes learnt through nurse education. Nursing is a demanding job and students have to learn to cope with outside life pressures whilst at the same time functioning effectively within their nursing role. Learning to cope with multiple pressures helps to prepare them for their future roles as qualified nurses.

Classification of curricula

There are many ways of classifying curricula. Four generally accepted descriptions are:

1. *The official curriculum.* This is the laid down policy of the school. It reflects the statutory requirements of training.
2. *The formal curriculum.* This is the learning planned by the school. The detailed syllabus, allocation programme and selection of teaching strategies all contribute to the formal curriculum.
3. *The actual curriculum.* This is the actual teaching and learning that takes place and may not reflect the official or formal curricula. The individual teacher will decide what is learnt. In this context the teacher is anyone

involved in teaching nurses, e.g. nurse teachers, nurse practitioners, other members of the health care team and also patients.

4. *The hidden curriculum.* This is the transmission of attitudes and values from teacher to student or from the wider context of the institution to its students. There are many hidden values in nursing which may influence the student.

The hidden curriculum is one of the most important aspects for those involved in nurse education to be aware of. Teachers transmit attitudes and values without being conscious of it. Enthusiastic tutors or practising nurses can influence students with an interest in what they are teaching. Students will model themselves on those around them and by the end of training they are likely to have developed the behaviours and beliefs of those they regard as ideal. These significant people may be labelled 'role models'. A role model may be one individual whom the student has admired and therefore modelled herself upon, or may be a collection of aspects of various people with whom the student has been in contact. It is also possible that they will have learnt from negative role models by making a decision never to act in the way that person does. The concept of role models may be deliberately applied by providing an appropriate person for the student to learn from, such as an experienced nurse as a mentor or clinical facilitator.

Disparity between values may occur as a result of the hidden curriculum. Students may experience the situation of a trained nurse saying 'You're not in the school now, on this ward you do it our way'. This transmits that education is of little value and may result in conflict for the student who feels that she ought to practise the way she has been taught by the school, but at the same time wants to be accepted as part of the ward team. This type of experience is called cognitive dissonance and was described by Festinger (1972) who defined it as:

> The feelings which an individual experiences as a result of perceiving inconsistencies between his values about something and his behaviour towards it.

The closer the relationship between theory and practice the less likely it is that such situations will be experienced. This demonstrates the importance of effective communication and positive working relationships between all those concerned in nurse education. Cork (1987) suggests that:

> Another approach to dealing with the 'hidden curriculum' is through the ongoing education of practitioners so that the values of the tutors and the values of the practitioners become more closely aligned.

The changing role of the nurse in response to technological advance and changing patterns of health and illness has already resulted in the innovation of speciality courses, particularly over the last two decades, and there would appear to be a recognition of the growing need for continuing education. The growth in size and remit of professional development teams reflects the increased need of continuing development of trained nurses.

Curricula models

Chapman (1985) defines the term model as 'a representation of reality, to enable us to understand something in real life'. Models are used in curriculum design to provide a structure enabling coherent development. Normally nurse education is based on an adaptation of a model developed in the general education system. Greaves (1984) says of nurse education:

> Previously in the United Kingdom no real use has been made of curriculum theory and practice, and there has been little in the way of objective thinking in curricular terms.

This statement reflects the way in which the nursing curriculum has developed. Initially nursing borrowed from other disciplines, such as medicine, by mimicking the presentation of knowledge and methods of achieving skills. Medical models tend to be disease orientated, emphasizing the presentation of disease, its investigation and medical treatment. Therefore learning nursing by this method tended to devalue nursing knowledge and skills as these were subsumed by medical knowledge and skills. The General Nursing Council for England and Wales, in its Educational Policy Document (1977), changed the emphasis of nurse education to a nursing model, recommending that the curriculum utilize a nursing process approach. It also prescribed an approach to curriculum planning which focused attention on the content of the curriculum. This was to be achieved by the use of behavioural ojectives which are statements of expected behaviour at the end of a learning experience. It is generally accepted that nurse training involves development of knowledge, skills and attitudes relevant to nursing. Writing a curriculum based on the objectives approach requires all three areas to be covered; in educational terms these are cognitive, psychomotor and affective. Jarvis and Gibson (1985) state that:

> The pre-specification of aims and objectives, or whatever terminology is employed, is the result of educators attempting to provide direction for the development of the curriculum at every level.

It is possible to write objectives in each of the three major areas. Taxonomies of educational objectives have been described which divide each of these areas into various levels of skill from basic to complex. In the cognitive or knowledge area Bloom et al. (1956) cited in Carrol et al. (1978) identified six levels as follows.

1. *Knowledge*: related to simple reproduction of facts.
2. *Comprehension*: understanding which can be demonstrated by the ability to explain meaning.
3. *Application*: the ability to apply knowledge to new situations.
4. *Analysis*: being able to break information down into its component parts, to clarify meaning.
5. *Synthesis*: being able to combine component parts to make a new whole.
6. *Evaluation*: the ability to make judgements using relative criteria.

In nurse education the cognitive area is perhaps the one which most lends itself to the use of educational objectives, although it may be criticized for being prescriptive and teacher-centred since it is likely to be the teacher who decides the objectives not the student.

Writing objectives for the psychomotor area is relevant to nursing because of the practical skills involved in learning to nurse. Fitts and Posner (1967) cited in Carrol et al. (1978) describe three phases in this area as follows.

1. *Cognitive phase.* This relates to knowing what to do. Carrol et al. (1978) suggest that a model of the required performance has to be remembered. Additional cognitive skills identified in this phase are as follows.
   (a) Knowing when to do the task.
   (b) Knowing when it is done.
   (c) Deciding what to do.
   (d) Knowing what to do.
   (e) Knowing why the task is being done in a specific manner.
   (f) Knowing how to communicate and report the task.
2. *Fixation phase.* This relates to practising the task that has been learnt. Manipulative skills are developed.
3. *Automation phase.* This occurs when a highly organized skilled performance can be demonstrated.

When writing objectives for psycho-motor skills all three of these phases should be considered.

The most difficult area to write objectives for is probably the affective one, since it is hard to describe observable behaviour related to attitudes and feelings. Krathwohl, Bloom et al. (1964) cited in Carrol et al. (1978) describe a taxonomy for this area with five levels:

1. *Receiving.* An awareness or willingness to pay attention toward something.
2. *Responding.* Response either by action or by experiencing a feeling.
3. *Valuing.* At this level there is acceptance or internalization of values and attitudes resulting in commitment.
4. *Organization.* This complex level allows the individual to select the most appropriate response in a situation where more than one response may be appropriate.
5. *Characterization.* At this highest level the individual's value system is characterized by consistent behavioural responses.

Teachers who are required to use an objectives approach can usefully apply the work of Bloom et al. However the effectiveness of this approach is dependent upon the teacher's expertise in writing relevant objectives at appropriate levels in the specific area of learning.

The development of nursing curricula models has also contributed towards curriculum development. These models usually incorporate elements of both general educational curricula models and also factors relevant to nursing. Greaves

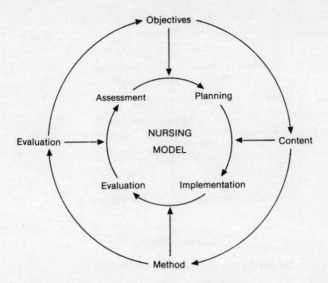

Fig. 4.1 An eclectic model of curriculum: after Greaves (1984)

(1984) describes an eclectic curriculum model (Fig. 4.1) which combines a model of general education with the elements of the nursing process and incorporates a model relevant to nursing practice. This approach provides a general framework to determine specific requirements. The outer circle represents the general educational components and consists of four phases:

1. *Objectives*: these are statements of intent which define the purpose of the curriculum.
2. *Content*: the subject matter to be included is specified.
3. *Method*: identification is made of available learning experiences, which enables selection of appropriate teaching and learning strategies.
4. *Evaluation*: this determines how the curriculum is to be assessed for effectiveness.

The general educational components may be applied to all four stages of the nursing process by setting objectives identifying content, selecting appropriate learning strategies and methods of assessment in order to develop problem-solving skills.

Development of models of nursing has further enabled clarification of the role of the nurse. Pearson and Vaughn (1986) suggest the following advantages of basing nursing practice on an agreed model.

1. To provide consistency in the approach to care therefore enabling continuity of care provision.
2. To reduce conflict within teams of nurses.
3. To enable other members of the health care team such as medical staff,

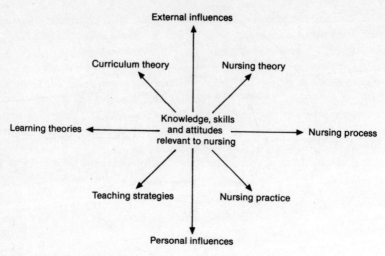

Fig. 4.2 Factors affecting the nursing curriculum: Gosby (1987)

paramedical and ancillary staff to understand the logic of nursing care.
4. To produce clear goals of nursing that can be understood by the whole team therefore giving direction.
5. To act as a basis for decision- and policy-making.
6. To enable identification of criteria for use in the selection of team members.

Greaves's eclectic model combining the general educational components, the nursing process stages and incorporating a nursing model of choice provides a sound framework for developing a nursing curriculum.

FACTORS AFFECTING CURRICULUM DEVELOPMENT

There is a considerable number of factors that affect the nursing curriculum (Fig. 4.2). The combined effect of all these influences will affect the knowledge, skills and attitudes gained throughout nurse education.

External influences
These include the statutory bodies, EC directives, professional organizations, government policies and the wider context of social factors for example patterns of health and disease, demographic changes and the changing economy.

The statutory bodies, EC directives and government policies influence the curriculum by specifying content, conditions and standards that must be met. In particular the change in control in July 1983 from the General Nursing Council for England and Wales to the United Kingdom Central Council for Nurses, Midwives and Health Visitors heralded a period of considerable change. The

UKCC set itself the task of examining nursing and nurse education. A series of consultation papers culminated in the publication of the report 'Project 2000' in May 1986 with recommendations, currently under discussion, which have implications for curricula change. Previously, 1985 had seen the publication of two other notable documents related to nursing and nurse education. These were the Royal College of Nursing publication *The Education of Nurses: A New Dispensation* and the English National Board consultation paper *Professional Education/Training Courses*. There was some similarity of thought related to the future development of nursing and nurse education.

The RCN publication had addressed as one of its issues the falling number of eighteen year olds available for recruitment to nursing and recommended that:

> Better training courses set in different learning environments would improve wastage, relieve the pressures on qualified staff to supervise and train rather than deliver care and enhance job satisfaction.

The ENB in its consultation paper had indentified a need to educate for the promotion of health and the prevention of disease rather than just to care for the sick stating that:

> The central role of professional nursing is to help and teach people to manage their own health more effectively, to raise the overall level of nursing ability within the community and to care directly for those people who would most benefit from professional nursing skills.

Project 2000 reflected the recommendations of both the preceding reports and following consultation with the profession published *Project Paper 9* in February 1987 which outlined the final proposals. These were:

1. *A single level of registered nurse.* The new nurse will be more actively involved in the delivery of care than at present and will not be simply someone who supervises it. Upon registration the new nurse will be able to practise in both non-institutional and institutional settings.
2. *Cessation of present trainings.* The existing trainings for first and second level nurses will end.
3. *Specialist practitioners.* Specialist practitioners will be persons with considerable experience as registered practitioners who will have completed additional education and training programmes. Some will be disease linked, others will represent specialist knowledge in nursing intervention or in health promotion. Specialist practitioners will combine teaching with practice.
4. *Helpers for nurses.* There will be a new range of helpers who should be supervised by and work under the direction of registered practitioners.
5. *A new educational framework.* Several factors are identified to include:
    5.1 *Supernumerary status.* Students would only provide a 20 per cent contribution to service in their three year period of initial education and training.
    5.2 *Improved teacher–student ratio.* A ratio of 1:12 is suggested.

5.3 *Appropriate education and re-orientation for teachers.* Ultimately all teachers should have degrees, though not necessarily in nursing.

5.4 *Student support in practice settings.* Those involved in teaching and supporting students in practice settings should be prepared for this role.

5.5 *Improved facilities.* Facilities provided within the NHS should reflect the better standards of higher education.

5.6 *Joint professional and academic validation.* This should be sought from the outset of change.

These proposals reflect consideration of the changing role of the nurse, the changing patterns of health and disease, demographic changes and economic and political factors as well as the more specific identification of problems within existing nurse education and training courses. Should the proposals be adopted the implications for change in the curriculum are considerable.

Curriculum theory

Curriculum theory developed within both general and nursing education is of value in design and development of the nursing curriculum. Sheahan (1980) identifies two broad approaches to curriculum theory. The first is the process model in which the criterion is the intrinsic value of the subject to be studied rather than content being selected with reference to student behaviour. This model would be difficult to apply to nurse education since there are specified goals which must be attained; the Nurses, Midwives and Health Visitors Act 1979 defined competencies that the nurse must attain throughout the process of her training course. Thus whilst it may be desirable that students gain an intrinsic value of nursing knowledge, the curricula approach also needs to be a practical one in enabling the student to achieve the required competencies. The second approach is the objectives model which provides clear educational goals, specifies behaviour, conditions and standards. Sheahan suggests that this approach is more relevant to nurse education. The curriculum theory at the basis of this approach has been described by Greaves (1984) who identifies four questions fundamental to the development of the curriculum. These are:

1. What is the curriculum's purpose?
2. What subject matter is to be used?
3. What learning experiences and school organization are to be provided?
4. How are the results to be assessed?

These questions focus attention on objectives, content, method and evaluation, the four general educational components incorporated in Greaves' eclectic model as previously described. Curriculum theory enables design and development of the curriculum.

Learning theories

There are various learning theories that may be considered when developing nursing curricula. Nurse education requires that both theoretical and practical skills be developed and that the student be able to relate theory to practice. Learning theories vary from simplistic to complex explanations of how learning takes place. Quinn (1980) identifies common theories and suggests how these may be applied to nurse education, as follows.

Stimulus–response theory. This theory suggests that behaviour occurs as a result of a stimulus. It can be applied to nurse education when learning practical skills by giving the students feedback on their performance thus reinforcing knowledge.

Cognitive theories. These theories are more concerned with the intellect and thinking skills. They can be applied to nurse education by helping students to organize the information they are receiving, presenting complete concepts or materials and identifying the relationships between component pieces of information.

Humanistic theories. These theories are more concerned with thinking, feeling and experiencing. The total experience is emphasized and importance is placed on teacher–student relationships and the learning climate. The theories are applied in nurse education by identifying individual needs of students and creating an environment conducive to personal development.

Social learning theory. This theory is concerned with the interaction between the individual and the environment. Learning is said to occur by observing the behaviour of other people. Application of this theory can be achieved by the provision of appropriate role-models, especially in the clinical environment.

Andragogical theory. This theory is based upon assumptions about how adults learn (described in Chapter Three). Application is achieved in developing students' ability to direct their own learning.

All of these learning theories can be usefully employed within the nursing curriculum; they should be selected according to the knowledge, skills and attitudes to be attained.

Teaching strategies

There is a wide variety of teaching and learning strategies that may be utilized in nurse education. Sheahan (1980) describes a continuum of teaching strategies which may be viewed as a stair (Fig. 4.3). On examination of this continuum it can be seen that methods move from dependent teacher-centred to independent student-centred. If one relates this to the ability and experience of the student it may be realistic to suggest that at the beginning of traditional training courses methods are more likely to be teacher-centred and that by the end of training methods are more likely to be student-centred. The nature of nursing is such that students need to learn in a safe environment how to take responsibility, make decisions and deal with stress. Experiential teaching methods allow the students to discover information for themselves and enable development of communication and interpersonal skills. The introduction of different styles of training courses such as the six pilot courses sponsored by the ENB may allow for a wider use of the strategies available. The proposals of Project 2000 would allow for more extensive use of student-centred strategies as students would be supernumerary. Current traditional schemes create the necessity to provide a safe student within the early stages of training so that she can fulfil her service commitment as soon as possible. This precludes the use of some of the more demanding and time consuming student-centred strategies.

Student-centred

Research

Projects

Individualized teaching: learning

Assignments

Case study

Teacher-led discussions: tutorials

Demonstrations

Lectures

Teacher-centred

Fig. 4.3 Continuum of teaching strategies: Sheahan (1980)

Nursing theory

Nursing theory cannot be considered in isolation from nursing practice, since nursing is essentially a practical application of knowledge. However no practical skill can be applied without having first given thought to what is required, how it is to be done and why it is to be done. Project 2000 identified that nurses need to be 'knowledgeable doers'. Developments in nurse education have reflected the need for integrating theory and practice, for example the move toward sequential teaching rather than blocks, and the introduction of clinical nurse teachers. Whilst both of these developments may be viewed as having improved the potential for relating theory to practice, neither appears to have resolved the problem fully. Greaves (1984) states that:

> In the development of a curriculum for nursing there is quite clearly a need for the relationship of theory to practice to be seen as equally important, interrelated and integrated into the very idea of nursing.

Margaret Alexander (1983) discusses the seclusion of tutors and of ward sisters into their respective environments of school and ward, and suggests that this may contribute to the disparate values between education and service. The integration of nurse teachers into the clinical environment and ward sisters into the school environment may decrease this disparity.

The body of knowledge related to nursing is growing as more nurses become involved in nursing research and in turn more practice is based on researched facts rather than traditional practices. Chapman (1985) defines theory as:

A proposed explanation of an event or series of happenings, often demonstrating the relationship of one to another. May or may not be proven.

She identifies that nursing theory may arise from deduction or induction. These processes are defined as:

Deduction – from another discipline i.e. something that works in one situation may be applied to another; and induction – producing theory out of practice by using the research process.

Previously it was identified that the nursing curriculum developed from knowledge transferred from other disciplines, therefore theory was deduced. The past two decades have seen a growth in nursing research, notably with the RCN series of studies, the development of the nursing process and of nursing models for care, resulting in a growth of inducted theory.

Nursing process

Kratz (1979) defines the nursing process as:

A problem solving approach to nursing, involving interaction with the patient, decision making and carrying out care based on the assessment of an individual patient's situation, followed by an evaluation of the effectiveness of our action.

The development of this systematic approach as a basis for nursing care has in turn enabled curriculum development.

Greaves (1984) suggests that the framework can be used at various levels from simple to complex.

1. *Simplistic application.* This enables care to be planned to suit the individual patient and also facilitates effective delivery of care; e.g. the use of standard care plans thus ensuring that all aspects of care are covered.
2. *Intermediary application.* This is at a more abstract level where a more in-depth assessment is carried out, and the subsequent analysis of the patient's actual and potential problems results in a comprehensive care plan.
3. *Advanced level.* This uses the nursing process as a theoretical frame of reference from which nursing care plans can be devised that reflect nursing theories of health and disease.

The adoption and implementation of the nursing process approach to care has not been an untroubled one. Lorraine Smith (1987) states that 'nurses felt that nursing process was being imposed rather than negotiated'. She argues that one factor in the non-acceptance of the nursing process may be that it is not a product of the United Kingdom and thus being foreign is viewed with suspicion. Smith also suggests that 'did not the introduction of nursing process imply, albeit indirectly, that nursing care was not all that it could be?' Despite these responses the nursing process has become an integral part of the nursing curriculum and its simplistic problem-solving approach provides an appropriate framework for assessing, planning, implementing and evaluating nursing care.

Nursing practice

Oliver D'A Slevin (1981) states that 'the nurse is becoming not only more of a nurse but more than a nurse'. The role of the nurse has changed over the past twenty years in response to advances in technology, increased knowledge, changing patterns of health and disease and an increased emphasis on the autonomous delivery of care by the nurse. Nursing practice influences the curriculum in several ways. The traditional training course exposes students to learning within the clinical environment for the major proportion of their time. However since the student is a necessary part of service provision it cannot be guaranteed that the learning environment will be an effective one.

Fretwell (1982) suggested that the apprenticeship system of nurse education was founded on two assumptions: that sisters and trained nurses teach in the ward and that student and pupil nurses learn as they work. Her research showed that most teaching related to technical aspects and that basic tasks were delegated to untrained nurses. She suggests that, 'the routinization of work contributes to an automatic job performance which removes the stimulation necessary to motivate the student to learn.'

This reasearch indicates that the current method of training nurses is inadequate to achieve the full potential from the educational experiences available, since the student is too tired or too busy to take full advantage of the opportunities that arise.

The quality of nursing practice will also influence the curriculum in that the higher the standard of care the better the learning environment is likely to be. There is an increased awareness of the need to examine standards of care and to be accountable. Alison Kitson (1987) examined raising standards of clinical practice as a fundamental issue of effective nursing practice. She suggests that standards of clinical practice should be scientifically validated and asks:

> It is not because nursing has relied far too long on intuition and experience rather than embracing more accepted scientific methodologies that it is now facing so many difficulties?

Whilst she recognizes that there is likely to be a deal of professional wisdom which should not be lost she also identifies that:

Nursing has suffered the double indignity of being dismissed as non-scientific and intuitive and discouraged from validating any of its basic notions on the grounds that what nursing dealt with did not require systematic investigation.

The increasing emphasis on research-based nursing practice and on measuring the quality of care influences the nursing curriculum by requiring both aspects to be included as formal elements of nurse education. These requirements are difficult to meet in the traditional training course because of its structure. Kitson identifies that:

> Education functions to equip practitioners with appropriate skills and knowledge; research solves difficult problems and opens up new areas of investigation; whilst the organisational structure ought to be geared to preserving the essential qualities of the therapeutic nurse–patient relationship.

The curriculum for nurse education needs to provide a learning environment in which the highest quality of nursing practice possible may be learnt and practised, giving due respect to research based knowledge whilst creating positive nurse–patient relationships.

The RCN (1987) in its recent publication makes a position statement on nursing. Nine key statements are identified of which three are of particular relevance to the nursing curriculum. The first states that:

> Nursing recognises its responsibility to society and individuals to provide a service which is client focussed, responsive to individual needs and is both effective and efficient.

This identifies the need to educate nurses to have problem-solving skills that will enhance an individualistic approach to patient care. The second statement concerns accountability stating that:

> Society and the individual can hold the nursing profession accountable for the quality of the service it delivers. The nursing profession accepts the responsibility to be held accountable for the quality of its service.

This statement raises the question of the position of the student nurse. One of the criteria relevant to this statement is that 'the nurse has a responsibility to refuse to care for a patient if she is not suitably qualified or competent to undertake the care'. The implications of this are for appropriate education and supervision of the student nurse in order that the patient receives the best standard of care. The third statement relates to safety in care provision stating that:

> The individual has the right to be provided with safe care, both physically and psychologically regardless of the context in which the nursing intervention takes place.

The implications for the curriculum relate to developing appropriate communication and inter-personal skills as well as the practical skills necessary for nursing practice.

Personal influences

The individual student is perhaps one of the most important factors to consider in relation to the curriculum. Despite similarities of entry conditions, learning experiences and assessment methods it is likely that there will be considerable variation in the performance and achievement of nursing students. This may be accounted for by their individual academic ability, their personality, the learning experiences to which they are exposed, their learning style, their relationship with their teachers, their health and their personal lives.

The nurse is an individual caring for individuals and as such needs to be prepared through nurse education to identify appropriate information, make appropriate decisions, take appropriate action and communicate appropriate information to those concerned. The importance of teaching problem-solving skills is therefore identified and thus if the need is for individual development of the student, in turn, it is necessary to identify their individual learning needs. Entwistle (1981) has identified particular characteristics for both students and teachers which affect learning.

Student characteristics
1. Previous knowledge.
2. Intellectual skills.
3. Types and levels of motivation.
4. Interests.
5. Levels of anxiety.
6. Preferred learning style.
7. Expectation about what is to be learnt.

Teacher characteristics
1. Expectations about students' previous knowledge and ability.
2. Enthusiasm.
3. Empathy.
4. Choice of course content and assessment.
5. Preferred teaching style.
6. Expectations about the level of outcome.

Entwistle suggests that the students' characteristics affect their perception of the learning task, and that teachers' characteristics affect the learning experiences they plan for achievement of the task. The two variables thus affect the actual process of learning and the final outcome which in turn may have an effect on the characteristics of either group, possibly bringing about change. The curriculum should aim at each student achieving her highest potential within the constraints imposed by the learning environment.

APPLICATION OF CURRICULUM THEORY IN THE CLINICAL ENVIRONMENT

One factor vital to the successful application of curriculum theory in the clinical environment is the relationship between the members of the teaching team. It is usual for a curriculum development group to consist of members from both the service and educational elements of nursing. If the curriculum is planned jointly then the aims will be mutually agreed and acceptable for both theory and practice. The notional teaching team consisting of practising nurses and nurse educators should decide how best to implement the curriculum in specific clinical environments. Greaves's eclectic model (1984) provides an illustrative example although in practice the curriculum development group should select the model which is most appropriate to its own environment and course.

Objectives
The objectives set for students in any clinical environment need to be relevant both to the student and the clinical speciality. The teaching team should decide exactly what they expect the student to learn during the allocation and write an agreed list of objectives which reflect the nursing process approach to care and reflect the nursing model utilized by the institution. These objectives should be presented to the students at commencement of the allocation and discussed with them so that there is a shared expectation of performance relevant to the student's ability and experience. Objectives stated in behavioural terms would enable identification of criteria for evaluation.

Content
The content of teaching and learning during the allocation needs to be specific to the clinical area. The team must be clear about potential learning within the environment and select relevant learning experiences that are achievable within the time available. This necessitates consideration of factors that affect the clinical environment such as the nature of the patient group, the physical environment, the ratio of trained staff to students, the ability and experience of both trained staff and students, the organization of care, communication channels and most importantly the attitudes of the clinical team toward teaching. There is little point in having an excellent teaching programme and insufficient staff to implement it. Each area will vary according to its specific make-up, thus two surgical wards whilst both labelled general may provide very different learning opportunities. This may be particularly affected by the leadership style of the ward sister as identified by Ogier (1980). It is important not to try to compete with similar clinical environments but to make the most effective use of your own clinical environment.

Methods

Methods used to enhance learning will relate to the resources available, both material and staffing, and also to the motivation and ability of those involved. There is a common misconception that learning only occurs when 'students' are sitting down having a 'teaching session'. Possibly the most important method of learning in the clinical environment is in the use of the 'role-models' as previously described. Providing appropriate supervision of students should automatically enhance the learning environment. Use should be made of natural learning opportunities, for example report time. This normal communication that occurs between nurses is a valuable learning opportunity if used effectively. The student should be encouraged to contribute to reporting with guidance on how to select and deliver relevant information. When planning a teaching programme it is a good idea first to identify natural learning opportunities such as doctors' rounds, case conferences and supervised practice, and to plan to make effective use of these. It is then possible to decide what supplementary teaching of a more formal nature is required. In this way a coherent teaching programme will be formulated that does not impose unreasonable pressures on either the students or staff involved in teaching them.

Evaluation

Evaluation by now should be a logical consequence if appropriate objectives have been set, appropriate content of learning been identified and relevant methods of teaching employed. Performance indicators may be set in that expectations of ability by the end of the experience should be easily identifiable in the objectives set, against which actual performance may be measured. Consideration must be given to the validity of these objectives in order to determine whether they have been set at an appropriate level related to the knowledge and experience of the individual student. It is relevant to decide who is to assess the student at the beginning of the allocation so that the assessor plans to have sufficient contact with the student throughout the experience in order to make the evaluation valid and reliable. It is also necessary to teach and develop assessment skills in those who are to be involved in evaluating student performance.

The nursing process

This component of the curricular model may be utilized in two ways, firstly as an approach to patient care and secondly as an approach to the individual student. When examining each phase of the nursing process the general educational elements of the model may be applied.

Objectives can be selected for assessment by deciding what you expect the students to be able to do, taking into acount their previous experience, current abilities and expected development. For example decide whether a first year student should be carrying out patient assessments, if so then the conditions for doing so must be defined:

1. How is she to learn?
2. Who is to supervise?
3. How will you know that the performance is satisfactory?

It must be acknowledged that she should not be assessing unsupervised, since if this is so it is tantamount to saying that one does not require a qualified nurse in order to carry out a nursing assessment. Having assessed the needs of the student you can then plan the teaching content, select teaching strategies and decide how you will evaluate the skill development, applying the four general curriculum elements to this phase of the nursing process. Similarly the format can be applied to the remaining three phases of the nursing process. It is important to remember not to expect each student to achieve the same level of performance within the same time span.

The nursing model
The model used in the clinical speciality can be used as a basis for teaching and learning at all times, whether formal or informal. Firstly, it is necessary to see that the permanent clinical team understand the philosophy of the model and how to implement it. It is pointless teaching the student the concept of a model in theory if this is not what they are going to experience in practice. Secondly, there is a need to decide how the student is going to learn to use the model. It is reasonable to expect that theory within the school will be based upon the selected model and that the student will have time to explore the theoretical concepts underpinning the model under the guidance of a qualified teacher. However, the actual practice of the model is likely to have the greatest impact with the student. Practising nurses can facilitate understanding by explaining how the model is implemented in practice and allowing the student to participate in implementation under supervision.

PLANNING A CLINICALLY-BASED TEACHING PROGRAMME

Elements of planning a teaching programme have already been discussed. It is a reasonable expectation of the school that each clinical area should have an organized teaching programme for students, allocated to them for experience. Utilizing the four component phases of the problem-solving approach, a checklist has been devised to aid development of a teaching programme.

1. Assessment

(a) *Students*
   (i) How many students need to be taught?

    (ii) What grade of students need to be taught?
    (iii) What is their previous theoretical experience?
    (iv) What is their previous clinical experience?
    (v) How long is their allocation?

(b) *Staff*
    (i) What is the ratio of trained staff to students?
    (ii) What is their level of experience?
    (iii) What professional development have they had?
    (iv) What is their level of motivation to teach?
    (v) What teaching experience have they had?
    (vi) What are their strengths and weaknesses?

(c) *The learning environment*
    (i) What can be particularly learnt in the clinical area?
    (ii) What are the natural learning experiences?
    (iii) What planned learning experiences would be useful?
    (iv) What are the constraints to learning?
    (v) What time is available for teaching.

2. Planning

(a) Identify learning needs which can be easily met.
(b) Identify how this is to be achieved and by whom.
(c) Identify learning needs which require more organization.
(d) Decide whether these needs can be met and if so how and by whom.
(e) Plan to allow for personal influences:
    (i) Motivation of the student.
    (ii) Motivation of the teacher.
    (iii) Pressures of workload.
    (iv) Ability of the student.
    (v) Ability of the teacher.
(f) Plan to use all available resources – material and human.
(g) Allow for influencing factors such as sickenss, annual leave, staff changes and high workloads.

3. Implementation

(a) Discuss the proposed programme with all those concerned.
(b) Identify the responsibilities of those to be involved in teaching.
(c) Identify mentors or facilitators to monitor the progress of individual students.
(d) Implement the teaching programme.

4. **Evaluation**

(a) Identify criteria that will let you know the student has achieved the desired level of performance.
(b) Decide who is to evaluate the student. This may be:
   (i) The student's mentor or facilitator.
   (ii) The ward sister.
   (iii) The clinically-based teacher.
   (iv) The student.
   (v) A combination of any of the above.
(c) Decide how the programme is to be evaluated.
(d) Decide who is to evaluate the programme. This may be:
   (i) The clinical staff.
   (ii) The clinically based teacher.
   (iii) The students.
   (iv) A combination of the above.
(e) Decide how evaluation data is to be kept.
(f) Decide how the programme is to be developed.

This check list will help to design a teaching programme. Remember that no two clinical areas would or should have identical programmes. The programme should be individually tailored to meet the needs of the students, the staff and the environment. It is also important to remember that not all staff like or want to teach, although it is a reasonable expectation of their role. This personal element may by overcome by using those who enjoy teaching, or who are more experienced, for the more formal aspects of the programme and those less inclined to teach, or who are less experienced, for the informal aspects. Be careful not to timetable the programme too tightly or you will not be able to fulfil it and both staff and students will become discontented. A good teaching programme will be dynamic not static, so regular review is vital. Change will stimulate, but do give the programme time to be effective before changing too much.

CONCLUSION

The nursing curriculum may be defined as a comprehensive concept relating to learning planned by the school which may be carried on in groups or individually, inside or outside the school. It is possible to classify the curriculum into subgroups of official, formal, actual and hidden. Nursing curricula are usually based on models which derive some elements from general curricular models and also include the nursing process approach to care, and may incorporate a specific nursing model. Models, which may be defined as representations of reality, are used in curriculum planning in order to provide a coherent structure to enable development. General curricular models usually have four components, these are objectives, content, methods and evaluations. These elements are cyclical in nature with evaluation leading to identification of further objectives thus facilitating development. Most nursing curricula use the 'objectives' approach which involves behavioural objectives. These are statements of expected outcome at the end of a learning experience. Taxonomies of behavioural objectives can be utilized to assist in writing appropriate objectives.

There are many factors that affect curriculum development, these may be external influences, personal influences, curriculum theory, learning theories, teaching strategies, nursing theory, nursing process and nursing practice. All of these factors need to be considered by curriculum development groups in order to achieve the most effective results within the constraints that exist.

The application of theory to practice is the true test of a curriculum. The aim of both practising nurses and nurse teachers should be to enable the student to attain the required competencies of nursing in the most effective manner, and also for her to achieve her full individual potential in order to become a practitioner capable of delivering high quality care and of taking on a leadership role within nursing practice. Applying curriculum theory to the clinical environment should enable the creation of a positive learning environment which generates satisfaction for all those working within it. The specific planning of a clinically based teaching programme will enhance the learning environment.

Knowledge of curriculum design and development enables practising nurses to contribute fully to nurse education and to make the most effective use of the learning experiences within their individual clinical speciality.

REFERENCES

Alexander, Margaret F. (1983). *Learning to Nurse*. London: Churchill Livingstone.

Carrol, A. D., Duggan, J. E. and Etchells, R. (1978). *Learning by Objectives: A Teachers Guide*. London: Hutchinson.

Chapman, Christine (1985). 'Curriculum design', *Senior Nurse,* Vol. 2, No. 7, pages 22–4.

Cork, N. M. (1987). 'Approaches to curriculum planning', in Davis, Bryn (eds), *Nursing Education: Research and Developments*. London: Croom Helm.

D'A Slevin, Oliver (1981). 'The changing role of the nurse', *Nurse Education Today*, August, pages 5–8.

Department of Health & Social Services (1979). The Nurses, Midwives and Health Visitors Act.

English National Board for Nursing, Midwifery and Health Visiting (1985). *Professional Education/Training Courses*. (Consultation Paper).

Entwistle, Noel (1983). *Styles of Learning and Teaching*. Chichester: Wiley and Sons.

Festinger, L. (1957). *A Theory of Cognitive Dissonance*. Illinois: Row and Peterson.

Fretwell, Joan (1982). *Ward Teaching and Learning*. London: Royal College of Nursing.

General Nursing Council for England and Wales (1977). Educational Policy Document.

Greaves, Fred (1984). *Nurse Education and the Curriculum*. London: Croom Helm.

Jarvis, Peter and Gibson, Sheila (1985). *The Teacher Practitioner in Nursing, Midwifery and Health Visiting*. London: Croom Helm.

Kitson, Alison L. (1987). 'Raising standards of clinical practice', *Journal of Advanced Nursing*, 12, pages 321-9.

Kratz, Charlotte R. (1979). *The Nursing Process*. London: Balliere Tindall.

Ogier, M. E. (1980). 'A study of the ward sister's leadership style and verbal interaction with nurse learners'. Unpublished PhD thesis, University of London.

Pearson, Alan and Vaughn, Barbara (1986). *Nursing Models for Practice*. London: Heinemann.

Quinn, Frances (1980). *The Principles and Practice of Nurse Education*. London: Croom Helm.

Royal College of Nursing (1985). *The Education of Nurses: A New Dispensation*. London: Royal College of Nursing.

Royal College of Nursing (1987). *In Pursuit of Excellence: A Position Statement on Nursing*. London: Royal College of Nursing.

Sheahan, John (1980). 'Some aspects of the teaching and learning of nursing', *Journal of Advanced Nursing*, 5, pages 491–511.

Smith, Lorraine (1987). 'Application of nursing models to a curriculum: some considerations', *Nurse Education Today*, 7, pages 109–15.

United Kingdom Central Council (1986). Project 2000. London: UKCC.

United Kingdom Central Council (1987). Project Paper 9, Project 2000: The Final Proposals. London: UKCC.

CHAPTER FIVE

DEVELOPING RESEARCH-BASED PRACTICE

INTRODUCTION

This chapter is intended to provide the reader with a brief overview of how and why nursing research evolved in the United Kingdom, and its application to the practice of nursing, thereby enabling the individual to judge the usefulness of evaluating and utilizing research findings to promote and develop professional practice. The term research is defined in this text as a process of systematic enquiry to facilitate the acquisition, assimilation and application of new knowledge.

RESEARCH

Evolution of nursing research in the United Kingdom

It is not necessary to delve very far into the archives of nursing history to find the milestones denoting the evolution of nursing research. It is less than forty years ago that Gladys Carter was appointed the first Boots Research Fellow in Nursing by the University of Edinburgh in 1953. The pioneering spirit of nurses like Gladys Carter, Doreen Norton, Marjorie Simpson and Winifred Raphael, provided the profession with a starting point for measuring and evaluating nursing.

In 1961 the Florence Nightingale International Foundation of the International Council of Nurses organized a conference in India. It was at this meeting that Dr. J. Brotherson (then Dean of the Medical Faculty at the University of Edinburgh) made reference to a paper published the previous year entitled, 'Research mindedness and the health professions' in *Learning to Investigate Problems* (Brotherson, 1960) when he stated that nursing must be a research-minded profession. However, apart from a small number of committed people, the impetus for nurses to become research-minded has been slow to gather momentum. Another milestone came in 1963, when Marjorie Simpson was appointed to the staff of the Chief Nursing Officer as Nursing Research Officer by the Ministry of Health in London. This appointment highlighted the growing importance now beginning to be attached by Government to developing a scientific approach to the investigating and measuring aspects of nursing.

From the late 1960s a number of major developments took place, which sought to increase awareness of the research process and its application to nurses and nursing practice.

Academic opportunities

Opportunities for nurses to undertake studies at a higher academic level increased considerably. Most significant was the inception of the Diploma and Degree in Nursing courses. Master degrees and doctoral studies also became part of the academic scene of nursing, albeit for the minority. The increase in educational opportunities provided a climate conducive to the development and awareness of the research and research skill.

The importance of developing research awareness amongst new entrants to the profession is one of the factors influencing curricula design (see Chapter Three). During the 1970s the Royal College of Nursing established a nursing care project which extended over a number of years and involved nurses from different nursing disciplines. This project provided the opportunity for a small group of nurses to develop research skills and make a valid contribution to nursing knowledge. The project results were produced as a series of twelve monographs which include studies on patient anxiety (Franklin, 1974); pre-operative fasting (Hamilton Smith, 1972); dressing technique (Hunt, 1975); and feeding unconscious patients (Jones, 1975). In addition, many of these studies now provide a point for further investigation by other researchers. The Royal College of Nursing now publishes a number of research projects under the following categories:

1. Nurse education.
2. Paediatric nursing.
3. Patient dependency and manpower.
4. Practice of nursing.
5. Primary health care.
6. Psychiatric nursing.
7. Ward sisters – role and function.

Other notable activities in the 1970s and 1980s include the establishment of nursing research units and the subsequent increase in research fellowship and studentship schemes. Three research units were established with the financial support of the Government; the Nursing Studies Research Unit, University of Edinburgh (1971); Nursing Education Research Unit, Chelsea College, University of London (1977); and the Nursing Practice Research Unit, Northwich Park Hospital and Clinical Research Centre (1979). Many other nursing research units were established during the 1970s and 1980s with funding from a variety of sources which include voluntary bodies, hospital boards, regional health authorities and the Department of Health and Social Security. Space precludes mentioning all those now established or the contribution that each has made towards generating a research based body of nursing knowledge.

Nurse education has been the focus for many of the early researchers, as demonstrated in Chapter One, many of whom adopted a sociological model to explain various aspects of nurse education, in particular, nurse wastage, recruitment, the relationship between nursing theory and practice, and measurement of clinical competencies. Hence, much of the research has tended to concentrate on nurses rather than on nursing (Auld, 1982) and has not always been conducted by nurses. The development of research skill by nurses has provided the opportunity for nurses to bring nursing research nearer to the practice of nursing. This development is partially due to the need for a sound scientific base and a well defined conceptual and theoretical framework for practice (Hockey, 1986). Further information is provided in Chapter Two on conceptual and theoretical frameworks.

The way in which nursing is organized and managed has also been the focus of investigation. An early study by Grant (1979), 'Time to care' examined the use of individualized patient nursing care plans for estimating workload. Many of the studies relating to nursing administration have also adopted a sociological model concentrating on people rather than their practice. This brief scenario of how research has developed in the United Kingdom, poses the question 'why has nursing research developed? Especially when so many nurses are unaware of such findings or how they should be used' (Hunt, 1984). The aim in the next section of this chapter is to summarize the main reasons why nursing research has evolved.

The value of research to nursing

Nursing is at a significant stage in its history. At no previous time has it been challenged so much or by so many from within or outside the profession. Over the years numerous changes in nursing practice, management and education have occurred, so that many people now openly challenge the status of nursing, its incumbents and their practices. If nursing is to be afforded the status of a profession, and its members recognized as professional practitioners, then they must as Boehm suggests participate in the scholarly and systematic demonstration of nursing practice through nursing research (Boehm, 1985). The only way that nurses can successfully meet the challenges that are being made is to adopt a research-based approach to their practice. This is not meant to suggest that all nurses should be involved in conducting research, (that should be the role of the nurse researchers), suffice that they seek to acquire, assimilate and apply relevant research findings as a basis for all nursing actions.

Research provides us the knowledge and framework to:

assess nursing problems or phenomena; find ways to improve nursing practice and patient care through creative studies; initiate and evaluate change; take action to make new knowledge useful in nursing.

(Adapted from Vreeland 1964).

The need to shift the emphasis in nursing practice from the traditional methods of trial and error, and authoritarianism towards an innovative and knowledge-based approach is of paramount importance, and is a change which Keighly (1984) considers would have been welcomed by Florence Nightingale, whose interest in having a factual basis for judgements is well-known.

Nursing, however, is in the words of John Wells a profession that dislikes innovation (Wells, 1980) and has not therefore always been rational in its approach to decision-making. Hence Virginia Henderson's well-known quote about nursing being a mixture of myth, mystery and magic still rings true in many areas of practice today (Keighly, 1984).

The momentum for all practising nurses to adopt a research-based approach to their work may be generated by the third item of the Code of Professional Conduct which clearly states that each registered nurse shall take every reasonable opportunity to maintain and improve professional knowledge and competence (UKCC 1984). With the increasing volume of research related knowledge from studies within a particular area of investigation, there now exist several reports which reveal similar findings in spite of using rather different methods and research subjects (Clarke, 1985). Such convergent results greatly increase confidence and validity of the research findings, and thus make failure to apply this knowledge indefensible if we are to comply with Item 3 of the Code of Professional Conduct.

The writings of Crane (1985) provide numerous references to support the need for nurses to promote actively the use of research findings in nursing practice. However, if nursing is to be research-based then every practising nurse must be knowledgeable about the work which has to be done and which is relevant to her field of practice (McFarlane, 1984). This process will ultimately require the nurse to analyse her current practices and knowledge base for those actions. In addition the skill to recognize the possibilities and need for subsequent change will become an essential competency for all nurses. Part of the learning process requires the nurse to know and understand the research process.

THE RESEARCH PROCESS

The research process consists of a series of logical steps that can be summarized under three main headings: designing, implementing, reporting/applying the findings.

Designing the research plan
1. Identify the problem to be studied.
2. Define the purpose of the study.
3. Search the literature.
4. Outline the population to be studied.
5. Specify the research hypothesis.
6. Re-examine the literature.
7. Gain access to the research setting.
8. Decide on the research approach.
9. Select or design the data collecting method(s).
   (a) observation.
   (b) interview.
   (c) survey/questionnaire.
   (d) experimentation.
10. Decide on the method of data analysis.
11. Select and contact the study sample.
12. Recognize and report the moral and ethical implications of the study and its limitations.
13. Conduct the pilot study, report the findings and make changes in the research design as applicable.

Implementing the research plan
1. Conduct the research according to the formulated plan.
2. Conduct, store and collate data according to the plan.

Reporting and applying the research
1. Prepare and write the research report.
2. Apply the results of the study.
3. Indicate areas for further study.

Fox (1976) has identified four main reasons why nurses undertake research: curiosity about research results; acquisition of an undertaking of the research process; acquisition of specific skills during the conduct of the research; and the partial fulfilment of the requirements for a course or degrees. Some nurses undertake research to obtain professional advancement, or as part of their employment contract.

Identifying the problem to be studied

The most likely sources of researchable problems are from nurses seeking to answer questions about their practices, or questions generated from reading research reports. Alternatively the need to test the propositions of nursing theory provides numerous research problems to be studied (see Chapter Two). Once the problem to be studied has been identified in broad terms, for example, the promotion of continence in elderly female patients, the subject area must be reduced to a manageable size. This is done by formulating a more specific question which is amenable to research. For example: Can pelvic floor exercises promote continence in elderly female patients who are incontinent?

This type of question could be studied. However, the next step in determining the researchability of a problem is to establish whether or not the patients and resources are available for study. Another fact that must be established before proceeding to the next stage of the process is the significance of the problem, in other words: Why is it important to conduct this study?

Defining the purpose of the study

The purpose of the study is usually defined in clear and concise statements and provides the focus and direction for the investigation. Actually defining the purpose can be one of the most difficult stages in the research process. If it is not done well the subsequent stages are likely to be even more difficult and can seriously affect the usefulness of the proposed study.

Searching the literature

Once the problem to be studied has been identified, and the purpose of the investigation clearly defined the next stage of the process is to search the literature. There are numerous reasons for conducting a literature search, as follows.

1. To enable the researcher to obtain and familiarize herself with the information currently available on the problem to be studied.
2. To enhance the researcher's knowledge of the subject area.
3. To help delineate the boundaries of the study.
4. To review the methods and findings of previous studies.
5. To provide contributory information from other sources to support and refute the research arguments.
6. To enable a relationship to be made between the present and previous studies of the problem.
7. To help formulate the expected contribution the study will make to the existing body of knowledge.
8. To provide a theoretical framework to the solution of the problem.

Sometimes a literature search generates only a small amount of information, if there has been little written on the subject previously. In some instances it is necessary to search the literature outside one's own discipline if suitable references are to be found. It is possible that a search can produce an overwhelming amount of literature on a particular subject. Hence, it is important to adopt a systematic approach when conducting a search, if vast amounts of valuable time are not to be lost. It is advisable for the potential researcher to formulate a series of questions pertaining to the literature required. It may be preferable to do this before going to a library, but some may find it useful to visit and talk with a librarian first.

These are typical questions that should be asked.

1. What information do I want the search to provide?
2. What answers do I want to find?
3. What time period is the literature to cover?
4. What are the geographical boundaries of the search to be (i.e. limited to United Kingdom only, or European as well)?
5. If the search is extended outside the United Kingdom, are papers other than those in English to be excluded or translated?
6. To what extent must I go outside nursing literature?
7. Are there limitations on the type of presentations of material (e.g. microfiche theses if machine for reading is not available)?
8. What type of library will be of most use?
9. Will I have access problems to certain libraries?

There are three main information sources, journals, bibliographies and reference books.

Nursing Journals can be subdivided into three main categories: abstracts, indices and awareness. There is only one British abstracting journal, the *Nursing Research Abstract* produced by the *Index of Nursing Research* at the DHSS and published quarterly. Abstracts provide a reference to monographs and journal articles in subject order and comprising a brief summary of the contents. There are three American indexing publications commonly available, the *International Nursing Index*, the *Index Medicus* and the *Cumulative Index to Nursing and Allied Health Literature*. The main aim of these journals is to provide a list of subject references to published articles. Awareness journals are a useful up-to-date reference of recent published articles and monographs. The Royal College of Midwives, the Health Visitors Association and the DHSS Library all provide current reference information, the one most nurses are perhaps familiar with being the *Nursing Bibliography*, published monthly by the Royal College of Nursing.

Bibliographies are concise and selective lists of information available on a specific subject. The Royal College of Nursing, the Royal College of Midwives, the DHSS and the Scottish Health Services Council (SHSC) all produce a wide variety of bibliographies covering a range of subjects. The Library Association publishes a bibliography of the nursing literature which most nurses are probably familiar with as it is widely available in libraries.

Reference books can be a useful source of information, as most libraries hold a range of these. The frequency of publication varies, for example the *Hospitals and Health Services Yearbook* is published annually. Another useful reference source is by access to international, national and local registers of research, however, only research that has been registered or recorded will be in evidence. A librarian will be the best person to advise on the usefulness and availability of research registers.

The thought of having to conduct a literature search can be a daunting experience even if the researcher is well prepared. By adopting a systematic approach to this stage of the research process, and seeking the advice of a librarian at the beginning of the project, the vast majority of pitfalls can be avoided.

The population to be studied

Delineating who is to be studied from the general population is initially determined by the purpose of the study. For example, you may wish to study patients who have had a myocardial infarction. These people are collectively referred to as the target population. It is from this group that you select your sample of people to participate in the study. If the study is to have credibility and allow for generalizations to be made, the sample must always be representative of the target population. Selection criteria can vary and are discussed below.

Specifying the research hypothesis

A research hypothesis is the term used to describe a clear, concise and unambiguous statement indicating the purpose of the study. Some researchers consider there is little difference between a research question and a research hypothesis. However, in practice a hypothesis tends to be more detailed and based on either induction or deduction. In other words, the hypothesis may be derived from a general idea which has been redefined to form a specific hypothesis for testing based on a theoretical framework (deduction). The theory is often generated by the literature search. Alternatively, the hypothesis may be based on observational findings which suggest that certain generalizations may be made (induction).

Hypotheses are often referred to as the researcher's working tools providing clear boundaries within which to operate. They are open to scrutiny, criticism and replication. Most hypotheses are written in the present tense, and usually indicate the target population. However, it is not always necessary to have formulated a hypothesis before conducting a research project. For example, those who undertake an ethnographic (described later in the chapter), or descriptive study to explain or describe a situation or event would not necessarily begin with a hypothesis. They would, however, have formulated research questions as guidance. Sometime researchers state the study hypothesis in terms that indicate there will be no significant difference as a result of a particular action or intervention. This type of statement is termed a 'null hypothesis' and can be either accepted or rejected.

Gaining access to the research setting

In order that the subjects of any research be protected, it is necessary for the researcher to produce a written protocol outlining details of the proposed study of submission to the senior staff of the establishment for environment involved. A protocol should include the following information:

1. What the research is about and how long it is expected to take.
2. Who the subjects are, and how they are to be selected.
3. Why it is necessary to undertake the study.
4. What the potential advantages and disadvantages of the study are.
5. How the research is to be conducted and by whom.
6 The qualifications of the researcher and her assistants to equip them to undertake the study.
7. How the research subjects are to be protected from harm and the methods for opting out of the study.
8. The methods used to report the findings and distribution of information.
9. How anonymity of the subjects or their environment is to be secured.
10. Approximate cost of the study and where the funds are to come from.
11. Copies of any questionnaires to be used.

In addition the researcher may have to present both herself and the protocol to the ethics committee, who will need to satisfy themselves that the research is justified and will cause no physical or pyschological harm to the subjects. The time gap between writing the proposal and actually gaining access to the research site and subjects can be quite considerable.

Deciding on the research approach

The decision as to the type of research design that is to be used to ensure that the research questions can be answered satisfactorily is determined to a great extent by the purpose of the study and the type of problem identified. It is not possible in one chapter to provide the reader with a detailed explanation of the various approaches to research, suggestions for further reading are therefore provided at the end of this chapter.

Approaches to research can be classified into two main categories, experimental or descriptive. The fundamental difference between these styles is the extent to which the variables can be controlled or manipulated by the researcher. For this explanation to be meaningful, it is necessary for the reader to understand the terms 'independent variable' and 'dependent variable'. A variable refers to any factor, attribute or characteristic, and may have different or changing values.

An independent variable is one that does not occur naturally in the study sample. It is introduced or manipulated by the researcher, whereas the dependent variable is the response or reaction by the subject to the introduction or manipulation of the independent variable, the effect of which can be observed by the researcher. Relationships between variables can be stated in various ways and are influenced by the type of research questions being investigated. For example, does giving an antiemetic pre-operatively cause a reduction in post-operative vomiting? The researcher could adopt an experimental approach to determine if the independent variable x (the antiemetic) causes an effect upon the dependent or y variable (the post-operative vomiting). The independent variable is controlled by the researcher, who is then able to make statements about the effect of x on y. Examples of studies that have used an experimental design include Hayward (1975) *Information – a Prescription against Pain* and Luker (1982) *Evaluating Health Visiting Practice.*

In situations where the researcher does not manipulate the independent variable, as in descriptive research, it is not possible to state that x had an effect on y, hence if changes occur simultaneously in more than one variable it may be possible to conclude that two or more variables are related. It may be appropriate in some situations to compare groups of subjects and their responses to a situation by using comparative statements.

Descriptive research aims to foster an understanding of situations, events or people by identifying the factors which exist and the relationship between them. The three main approaches under the heading of descriptive research are survey, case study and observation. Survey research is probably the most commonly used and enables information to be collected from a large sample, hence, results from surveys can often be generalized to the total population. However, care must be taken not to make generalizations if the sample is not statistically representative of a target population.

An example of a well-conducted survey is the study by Jill Rogers (1982) who sampled 3000 trained nurses who had completed a Joint Board of Clinical Nursing Studies certificate course, (now English National Board course). She ensured by her sampling technique (discussed later) that her sample included nurses who had completed different specialist courses, thus enabling her to generalize her findings to all nurses who have completed a certificate course with the JBCNS.

A case study approach is designed to allow for an in-depth investigation of a specific individual, community, family or event, in order to understand the characteristics involved. Examples of this approach include the study by Kogan and Henkel (1983) on the observations of civil servants, health authority representatives and researchers.

Observational studies are sometimes referred to as an ethnographic approach to research, based on the work of anthropologists who gained entry to various communities in order to study their characteristics by observation. This type of approach is favoured by many nurse researchers who wish to understand and describe a particular clinical situation or group of people, and has formed the basis for much of the research into clinical practice and practitioners.

As each research approach has its advantages and disadvantages, researchers often use a combination of methodologies to answer different types of research questions contained within a particular study. For example, Desmond Cormacks's study – 'Psychiatric nursing observed' – used participant observation to observe what the nurses did, and a questionnaire and semi-structured

Table 5.1 Summary of main strengths and weaknesses

Research Style	Strengths	Weaknesses
Ethnography	Rich source of qualitative data High content validity High ecological validity	Low reliability Time consuming Low internal validity Low population validity Qualitative data may be difficult to analyze
Survey	High construct validity High reliability High population validity Data often numerical and easy to analyze	Low ecological validity May be low content validity
Experimental	High reliability High construct validity High internal validity Data numerical and easy to analyze	Low ecological validity Often low population validity Low content validity

interviews to ascertain information from patients.

A summary of the main strengths and weaknesses of the three popular research approaches is given in Table 5.1.

A brief explanation of the terms reliability and validity is provided for those unfamiliar with the terminology.

Reliability is the first basic characteristic every instrument of measurement must possess. It refers to the instrument's level of consistency and repeatability. In other words, it must be capable of producing identical data when administered in the same circumstances on two or more occasions.

Validity is the second essential characteristic of an instrument and refers to whether or not the instrument measures what it purports to.

The extent of an instrument's reliability and validity can be determined in a number of ways. For example, to test reliability one can use the test/retest method. This requires the instrument to be tested on a group of subjects, then retested after an interval has elapsed. The two sets of data are then compared. This test is more appropriate for instruments designed to measure or elicit information of a stable nature, as the interval gap may result in low reliability if used on instruments designed to measure rapid change

Another test is the alternative form or interrelated test. With this form of testing the researcher develops two different forms of the instrument and administers both to one group on the same occasion. This produces two sets of data for comparison.

A third test is the split half procedure. Unlike the previous tests this requires only one test and one group of subjects. However, the scoring system is designed still to produce two sets of data for comparison to determine whether or not a correlation or relationship exists. This procedure is sometimes called the odd-event test, as the items for testing can be categorized into odd and even numbers and a score for each obtained.

A fourth type of test is the Kuder-Richardson, this test is designed to estimate the relationship of the response pattern to each separate item to the data from performance on the total instrument (Fox, 1976).

The extend to which an instrument has validity can be determined in numerous ways. Researchers often refer to the validity procedures in order of their strength. For example, face validity is the weakest, and is applied when an instrument appears on superficial examination to measure what it is intended to. Content validity is considered by some researchers to be equated with face validity, but there are convincing arguments to support the view that content validity can be a stronger indicator than face validity. For example, the researcher may ensure that the items comprising the measure represent a reasonable sampling of all the possible items or behaviour that make up the situation being measured.

The validity of an instrument is greatly enhanced if procedures used have an empirical basis, for example, construct, concurrent and predictive validity each require some alternative criteria to judge the validity of the instrument against.

Construct validity can be established within a single study; it requires the researcher to formulate a hypothesis based on theory about characteristics of those who have high scores on a test (compared to those with low scores) and then test them (Shelley, 1984).

Concurrent or criterion-related validity requires the researcher to present correlated data indicating the extent to which his instrument correlated with some already existing and accepted measure of the characteristic. Predictive validity is probably the strongest of those mentioned and is demonstrated by the forcefulness of the researcher's argument about his instrument's predictions of the respondents' future behaviour.

Researchers often use the terms internal and external validity. Internal validity is concerned with the properties of the measuring instrument. External validity is concerned with making generalizations. For example, can the research findings be generalized to groups other than those involved in the study (population validity), or other situations or settings (ecological validity)?

Figure 5.1 provides a clear indication of the relationship between validity and reliability and the different research styles.

THE DATA

Selecting or designing the data collecting method(s)

The basis for selection and design of the data collecting method(s) relates to the type of research approach that is to be used, and the appropriateness of each type of method to the particular study. An in-depth discussion on each of the available methods is not feasible in a book of this nature; the reader is therefore directed to the references at the end of this chapter.

Research is, as I am sure you are now fully aware, about asking questions. The researcher, in deciding on the method of data collection, takes account of what is to be asked, to whom, and how the sample for the study is to be selected. As mentioned previously, some researchers use a variety of instruments to answer different types of question within a particular study. The most commonly used methods in nursing are observation, interview, questionnaire and activity sampling.

Data analysis

An essential pre-requisite of data analysis is knowing how the data are to be summarized, interpreted and reported. For example, are data amenable to statistical analysis? The data must be organized in a way that is meaningful to researchers. Space precludes providing the reader with details of the various methods of data anlaysis; however, references provided at the end of the chapter offer a starting point.

Selecting and contacting the study sample

Target populations are groups that the researcher wished to generalize her findings to. Hence, the importance of selecting a representative sample from the total study population. For example, if everyone in the target population has an equal chance of selection, the term given to the sampling procedure is 'simple random sampling'. If, on the other hand, the researcher decides to select every third or fifth subject from the study population, this is termed 'systematic sampling'.

In studies like Rogers (1982) who sampled a number of subjects who had completed different JBCNS courses, the sample is referred to as a 'stratified random sample'. In other words, the sample has been randomized according to some additional factor(s) i.e. different types of courses.

When a researcher wants to sample from a wide geographical area, it is possible to do this in stages using a technique called 'cluster' or 'multistage sampling'. For example, the treatment of patients who have had a myocardial infarction, the first stage of the sampling procedure is to select at random a pre-determined number of hospitals, then to select at random patients from each hospital.

The above methods of sampling all relate to subjects who have an equal chance of selection. The next section briefly mentions sampling techniques that can be used when the probability of selection is unequal or unknown. For example. convenience sampling is when a subject is in the right place at the right time. The researcher may select the first fifteen female patients attending a hospital outpatients department. Alternatively, the researcher may decide to include male patients in the sample, or to use 'matched pairs' (subjects that have certain pre-set characteristics).

The term 'quota sampling' is applied to the study subject selected according to number required in each category. The study sample could be selected on the basis that the subject appears to be representative of a pre-determined criterion, this is termed 'purposive sampling'. Finally, selection could be arbitrary as opposed to random sampling. For example, select two wards from a list of ten. The method for contacting the subjects and gaining their co-operation will vary according to the type of study being undertaken. Some subjects may be sent written communications asking them to participate, others may receive a verbal request. The time span between seeking co-operation and commencing the study will also vary from weeks to perhaps a few moments.

Moral and ethical considerations

To be of value, nursing research involves closely scrutinizing the activities, behaviour and experiences of others. It is the very nature of research which raises numerous moral and ethical questions. With respect to human rights, legal accountability focuses upon evidence that the professional practitioner or researcher has not failed his/her responsibility by either intentionally or unintentionally withholding relevant information that might have altered the patient or subject's decision. Knowledge about the changing scope of nursing responsibility and emerging ethical issues affecting all practitioners in health care today is a necessary requirement for professional nursing practice in which accountability for the protection of human rights of consumers is accepted, (American Nurses Association, 1975). By entering into a fieldwork situation the researcher becomes part of that setting and is exposed to all aspects of the environment. Even if those aspects from which the moral or ethical dilemmas arise are not part of the research study, the researcher by virtue of being present and a witness has a responsibility to the participants (Field and Morse, 1985).

Guidance for nurses who undertake research, or who are in positions of authority where research is to be carried out, or practising in areas where research is being conducted, are provided by the Royal College of Nursing in a booklet entitled 'Ethics related to research in nursing' (RCN, 1977). A patient can, however, only give informed consent if he/she is able to exercise free power of choice without undue inducement or any element of force, fraud, deceit, duress or other forms of constraint or coercion (Annas, Glantz and Kratz, 1977). Implied consent can be deemed given if the individual is sent a questionnaire and sends it back completed. All research subjects or their legally authorized representatives should clearly understand the following:

1. The purpose of the study and how it is to be conducted.
2. Any risks however slight which might be involved.
3. The benefits of participating.
4. Methods applied to protect anonymity of subjects.
5. Who will have access to raw data and completed research findings.

6. Methods of opting out of the study.
7. Their right to question the researcher.

All research that involves human subjects should be approved by an ethical committee whose function is to ensure the protection of potential research subjects. Ultimately, however, it must be the individual nurse researcher's sensitivity to the moral implications of research combined with a firm adherence to the professional code of practice that ensures the security and well-being of all who participate in research.

Pilot study

A pilot study is an exact, but small-scale, replica of the main study. The purpose of a pilot study is to 'test out' the proposed methodology and identify its strengths and weaknesses. The study sample subjects should have the same characteristics as those selected for the main study. If changes have to be made as a result of the pilot study, it may be necessary to do a second study, before undertaking the main research. It is not, however, always necessary to conduct a pilot study, especially if the methodology and measuring instruments are familiar to the researcher and have been used on a similar study sample.

The main study

Once any pilot study has been completed the main research study should commence. It is important that the researcher implements the plan for data collection and analysis as indicated in the proposals. The degree of research control over variables will depend on the research approach adopted as previously discussed.

Writing the research report

The final stage of the research process is writing the research report. Although research reports usually follow a standardized format, they are often difficult to write and many more hours can be spent thinking about getting started than it usually takes actually to write the report. As in keeping with other stages of the research, it is beneficial to approach writing in a systematic way.

The purpose of the research report is primarily one of communication. By providing details of the study, it enables others to do the following:

1. Examine the findings and methodologies used.
2. Build on existing knowledge.
3. Extrapolate implications for nursing practice, education or management.
4. Replicate the study.

A research report usually presents information in the following sequence.

1. Abstract of the research.
2. Introduction – includes problem to be studied.
3. Literature search – the findings in relation to the study.
4. Design and conduct of the study.
5. Analysis of data and findings.
6. Discussion, conclusions and limitations of the study.
7. References cited in the report.
8. Appendices – includes copies of instruments used.

Evaluation

The importance of evaluation is discussed in Chapter Six, but it is the intention in this section to provide the reader with a checklist that may help to determine the value of the research to a given situation. The evaluator should adopt a systematic approach when reading a research report. It is always useful to commence this activity by ascertaining the qualifications and background of the researcher and his suitability to conduct research.

Next, establish what the report is about; this can usually be done from reading the abstract. The title of the project ought to indicate the boundaries of the study. There should be a clear and concise statement to indicate the purpose of the investigation and the justification for doing it. The literature search should indicate previous studies and their relationship to the present study in detail. If the study requires a hypothesis to be used, did it generate from the literature search, and is it clearly stated? The methodology must state the following:

1. Type of research approach used.
2. Details of the information required and relevant variables.
3. Sample population and method of selection.
4. Data collection techniques.
5. Method of data anlaysis.

The findings should be presented in a clear and unambiguous manner, and must relate to the data collected and research questions.

Any conclusions, inferences or recommendations should be substantiated by the research findings and not merely implied. Does the research indicate the limitations of the study, and are further questions for investigation generated? What new knowledge has been gained from reading the study, and are suggestions made to indicate how the findings can be incorporated into clinical practice?

THE APPLICATION OF RESEARCH IN PRACTICE

At the beginning of this chapter, research was defined as the acquisition, assimiliation and application of new knowledge. However, over time it has become evident that even with increased production of policy-related knowledge and improved technological procedures for transfer and dissemination, 'the frequency of use and impact of knowledge has not increased substantively' (Caplan, 1980).

Research findings suggest a variety of reasons for nurses not using research findings which include lack of knowledge on how to do the following:

1. Gain access to research based literature, (Kelefian 1975, Kirchhoff 1982, C.U.R.N. 1983, Hunt 1984).
2. Select research findings for use in clinical practice,(C.U.R.N. 1983, Kreuger et al. 1978).
3. Interpret and utilize research findings, (C.U.R.N. 1983, Krueger et al. 1985).

There is also misunderstanding about who should be responsible for selecting and transforming research-based knowledge into a format and idiom appropriate for use in a particular situation, (C.U.R.N. 1983, King et al., 1981, Horsley et al., 1978).

It has been suggested that lack of explicit and effective instruction regarding utilization of research in practice constitutes a major barrier (Horsley, 1985). However, even when information is timely, relevant, objective and given to the right people in a usable form, its use has not, according to Caplan (1980) been guaranteed. Strategies are therefore required to bridge the gap between the research findings which are available and their utilization in practice. These are essential if nursing is to become a knowledge-based profession.

Various models have been developed to promote the utilization of research. An article by Joyce Crane (1985) provides an overview of four models applicable for promoting the application of research in practice settings, as follows:

1. The research, development and diffusion model.
2. The social interaction and diffusion model.
3. The problem solving model.
4. The linkage model.

The research, development and diffusion model has been widely used in America. The model is based on the assumption that the target population can be easily and effectively reached via a complex system of information dissemination. Adoption is expected to occur naturally over time. The researchers do not necessarily use the 'consumers' needs' as the primary motivation for generating new knowledge. In the light of findings by Clarke (1985) and Caplan (1980) that uptake of relevant findings even when presented in a usable format does not occur, the criticism of this model is possibly self-evident. Crane provides several critical references to this model.

The social interaction and diffusion model is described by Crane as specifying the following:

1. Stages in the innovation process and the relative importance of various channels at each stage.

2. Ways in which perceived characteristics of innovations influence their rate of adoption.
3. Characteristics of early and late adopters.
4. The role of opinion leaders in diffusing innovations.
5. Factors in the relative success of change agents attempting to influence the diffusion process.

This model, as is evident by its structure, attempts to account for the way innovations diffuse throught a social system. Its critics argue that is has not taken account of problems that arise when attempting to implement change in an organized social system.

The problem-solving model is described as a user-orientated approach, which incorporates a sequence of activities with the following stages:

1. Diagnosis and statement of a problem.
2. Search and retrieval activities to find a solution (innovation).
3. Adapting the innovation to meet user needs.
4. Implementing the innovation.
5. Evaluating the effectiveness.

The main criticisms of this model are its emphasis and reliance on user initiation and application, and weak strategy for wider dissemination. In addition, there appears no compulsion on the user to incorporate research-based findings.

The linkage model has been developed to incorporate the strengths of the three previous models into a single perspective thereby linking together the users, resources, solutions and dissemination strategy. The four component parts are all inter-related.

1. Users with identified needs and a system for problem-solving combined with a willingness to try out and share new ideas with others.
2. A resource that generates new ideas and develops new knowledge to find solutions to user problems.
3. A mechanism to transmit problems and solutions between interested parties and feed back to the resource system.
4. A mechanism that effectively transforms and disseminates new knowledge etc. back to the user system from the resource.

The main criticism of this model appears to be the minimal extent to which there has been empircal testing of the model (Crane, 1985).

CONCLUSION

Using research findings as a basis for clinical practice has obvious implications for nurse education. The argument for research-based knowledge and new technologies to be incorporated in both basic and post-basic nursing curricula is self-evident if schools of nursing are to meet their responsibilities of preparing nurses to become 'knowledgeable doers'. It is through the facilitative skills (Chapter Eight) of teachers and practitioners that new knowledge can be disseminated, assimilated and utilized in practice.

REFERENCES AND SUGGESTED FURTHER READING

American Nurses Association Commission of Nursing Research (1975). *Human Rights Guidelines for Nurses in Clinical and Other Research,* Kansas City Mo: American Nurses Association Publication No. 0–46, 1–11.

Annas, G. J., Glantz, L. H. and Kratz B. F. (1977). *Informed Consent to Human Experimentation – The Subject's Dilemma.* Cambridge, Massachusetts: Ballingers.

Auld, M. G. (1982). A Theme for the Future – Research a Base for the Future. Research Conference Proceedings, University of Edinburgh Nursing Studies Unit.

Boehm, S. (1985). 'Research as a basis for changing nursing practice', *Topics in Clinical Nursing,* July, Vol. 7, Part 2, pages 39–44.

Bond, S. (1983). 'Promoting research utilisation through information services' in *Research into Nurse Education,* B. D. Davis (ed.). London: Croom Helm.

Brotherson, J. H. (1960). 'Research mindedness and the health professions' in *Learning to Investigate Problems.* Geneva: International Council of Nurses and Florence Nightingale Foundation.

Caplan, N. (1980). 'What do we know?'

Clarke, M. (1985). 'The use of research reports in planning', 'Continuing education for trained nurses', *Journal of Advanced Nursing* 10, pages 475–82.

Cormack, D. F. S. (1984). *The Research Process in Nursing.* Oxford: Blackwell Scientific Publications.

Crane, J. (1985). 'Using research in practice – research utilisation: theoretical perspectives', *Western Journal of Nursing Research,* May, Vol. 7, No. 2, pages 261–8.

Curn Project (1983). *Using Research to Improve Nursing Practice: A Guide.* New York: Grune & Stratton.

Davis, B. D. (1984). *Research into Nurse Education.* London: Croom Helm.

Field, P. A., and Morse, J. M. (1985). *Nursing Research – The Application of Qualitative Approaches.* London: Croom Helm.

Fox, D. J. (1976). *Fundamentals of Research in Nursing.* New York: Appleton-Century-Crofts.

Grant, N. K. (1979). *Time to Care.* London: Royal College of Nursing.

Hamilton Smith, S. (1972). *Nil by Mouth.* London: Royal College of Nursing.

Haughey, B. P. (1984). 'Considerations in applying research findings to practice' in *Dimensions of Critical Care Nursing,* Sept/Oct, Vol 3, No 5, pages 288–92.

Hayward, J. (1975). *Information – a Prescription Against Pain.* London: Royal College of Nursing.

Hockey, L. (1986). 'Nursing in the United Kingdom – the state of the art' in *International Issues in Nursing Research,* Stinson, S. M. and Kerr, J. C., (eds). London: Croom Helm.

Horsley, J. A. (1985). 'Using research in practice – the current context', *Western Journal of Nursing Research,* Feb., Vol. 7, No. 1.

Hunt, J. (1984). 'Why don't nurses use these findings?', *Nursing Mirror,* Feb. 22, Vol. 158, No. 8.

Jones, D. (1975). *Food for Thought.* London: Royal College of Nursing.

Keighley T. (1984). 'How vital are statistics?', *Nursing Times* 80 (44), Oct. 31, pages 18–19.

Kelefian, S. (1975). 'Problems in the dissemination and utilisation of scientific knowledge – how can the gap be bridged?' in Ketefian, S. Translation of theory into nursing practice and education, Proceedings of the Seventh Annual Clinical Sessions, pages 10–31. New York: New York University.

King, D., Barnard, K. E., Hoehm, R. (1981). 'Disseminating the results of nursing research', Nursing Outlook, 29, pages 164–9.

Kirchoff, K. T. (1984). 'Using research in practice', 'Teaching research utilisation', Western Journal of Nursing Research, 6, pages 265–7.

Krueger, J. C., Nelson, A. H., Wolanin, M. O. (1978). Nursing Research: Development, Collaboration and Utilisation. Germantown M. D.: Aspen System Corporation.

Luker, K. (1982). Evaluating Health Visiting Practices. London: Royal College of Nursing.

Miller, J. R., and Messenger, S. R. (1978). 'Obstacles to applying nursing research findings', Americal Journal of Nursing, 78, pages 632–4.

Rogers, J. (1982). The Follow-Up Study – Career Patterns of Nurses Who Completed a Joint Board of Clinical Studies Certificate Course, Report to DHSS. London: DHSS.

Royal College of Nursing (1977). Ethics Related to Research in Nursing. London: Royal College of Nursing.

Shelley, S. I. (1984). Research Methods in Nursing and Health. London: Little, Brown & Company, Churchill Livingstone.

Stelter, C. B., and Marran, G. (1976). 'Evaluating research findings for applicability in practice', Nursing Outlook, 24, pages 259–63.

Stinson, S. M., Kerr, J. C. (1986). International Issues in Nursing Research. London: Croom Helm.

Treece E. W., Treece J. W., Jr. (1982). Elements in Nursing. London: C. V. Mosby Company.

Vreeland, E. M. (1964). 'Nursing research programmes of the public health service', Nursing Research, 13, page 148.

Wells, J. C. A. (1980). Nursing, a profession that dislikes innovation: an investigation of the reasons why, MA Thesis, Brunel University.

Wilson-Barnett, J. (1983). Nursing Research – Ten Studies in Patient Care. Chichester: John Wiley & Sons.

United Kingdom Central Council (1984). 'Code of professional conduct', UKCC.

CHAPTER SIX

EVALUATING NURSE EDUCATION

INTRODUCTION

Teachers and clinical supervisors have a duty to consider critically all aspects of the curriculum that contribute to student learning. In this way, both strengths and weaknesses can be highlighted and action taken to enhance those experiences which have proven successful and to remedy those which have been deficient. This responsibility rests with all those who contribute to nurse education programmes, but reference to the specific duties of individuals is addressed later in this chapter.

The concept of evaluation will not be new to readers who are no doubt aware of the significance of evaluation in nursing care delivery, an activity discussed in Chapter Two. The concept is now pervasive in nursing and applies not only to individual patient care but also to the assurance of quality nursing services and the maintenance of professional standards. Evaluation at both these levels involves a process of assessment or re-assessment.

To a certain extent the same principles apply to evaluation in education, but for purposes of clarity the terms evaluation and assessment are used in a virtually exclusive manner. In the United Kingdom it is customary to draw a distinction between the terms, but this is not always the case in North American literature. There, the term evaluation is frequently used to denote what we refer to as assessment.

EVALUATION

Defining evaluation

The English National Board for Nursing, Midwifery and Health Visiting defines evaluation as 'the collection and use of information in order to make decisions about an educational programme' (ENB, undated).

The important point to make is that this distinguishes evaluation from assessment, which the ENB defines as 'the procedure by which a student is judged to have achieved the standard required for qualification' (Harrison R., 1984, cited in ENB, 1987). Assessment then, is concerned with measuring a student's

Evaluation	The value of learning experiences and the course overall
Assessment	A measure of student competence and progress

Fig. 6.1 Distinguishing evaluation and assessment

competence and progress and is discussed in detail in Chapter Nine. Evaluation is the process by which educational experiences, and the course overall, is judged to be of value (Fig. 6.1) and its purpose is to provide information that can be utilized to effect development and improvement of the educational experience or course. Although the means by which information is gained to assess competence or to evaluate the course is often the same, the purpose of each differs.

The key characteristics of evaluation are that it should be,

planned, systematic, focused and utilized.

Again, this is not dissimilar to the requirements of patient care evaluation, and the weaknesses in the execution of educational evaluation are often a reflection of those evident in reviews of the implementation of the nursing process.

Planned evaluation
Evaluation which occurs spontaneously or fortuitously is unlikely to yield the breadth or depth of information that is required in order to make valid decisions about the learning experience under review. Just as the planning of aims, objectives, content, method and assessment are stressed, so too is the significance of devising in advance a framework for evaluating these components. This applies equally to the level of curriculum or whole course design, as it does to the level of clinical supervision or opportunist learning in practice settings. The means by which clinical supervisors can plan a framework to evaluate clinically-based teaching and learning is discussed later in this chapter.

Systematic evaluation
The importance of devising a scheme which addresses the issues it seeks to review in a structured and sequential fashion, has its reward when the information is collated to provide the basis for decisions on development and improvement of the learning experience. A systematic approach to evaluation is developed as an exemplar in the final section of this chapter.

Focused evaluation
Planned, systematic evaluation is likely to yield information about those aspects of the learning experience which are most important, but this is not necessarily the case. The methods used may also increase or diminish the likelihood that critical areas will be avoided or 'difficult' dimensions ignored.

Focused evaluation is concerned with ensuring that in devising an evaluation framework those areas which are most important in determining learning outcomes are included in the scheme in such a way as to encourage an adequate response. Clearly, in clinical learning situations (as in all teacher-learner transactions), inter-personal relations are crucial, yet if clinical supervisors are unsure of their role and lack confidence they may consciously or unconsciously deny students an opportunity to focus on this critical element in the process.

Utilized evaluation

The *raison d'être* of evaluation is to develop and improve learning experiences, yet the characteristic most often ignored is that of utilization. In the clinical situation, reviewing the learning experience at the end of a placement with students often becomes simply a ritualized questioning. It is often only too evident to the students that their comments and observations serve no more purpose than the moves in a 'closure game' to terminate the placement.

This situation is also true of short and long courses where evaluation is scheduled for a limited period on the last day and serves to round off the proceedings. The information collected may remain uncollated and unanalysed, or simply reported upon briefly with little intention of utilization to effect change. These rituals have been discussed more fully elsewhere (Esterbury-Smith & Tanton, 1985).

A major step towards enhancing the meaningfulness and utility of evaluation is to employ both formative and summative evaluation. Inevitably there are elements of learning experiences, not least outcome or achievement of objectives, which cannot be evaluated until the end of the course (or often more realistically much later), dictating a summative or terminal approach. However, evaluating learning experiences as they progress enables those minor modifications to structure and process that can be made during the experience to be initiated for the benefit of current students. Formative evaluation of this nature diminishes the often perceived futility of terminal evaluation (see Fig. 6.2).

Formative evaluation	**throughout** the course or learning experience
Summative evaluation	at the **end** of the course or learning experience

Fig. 6.2 Distinguishing formative and summative evaluation

Above all, planned, systematic and focused evaluation, if utilized, serves both to enhance the educational experiences available to the students and to promote the professional development of teachers and clinical supervisors through a process of critical reflection.

WHAT SHOULD BE EVALUATED?

It is tempting at this point to say everything. But this would do little other than to emphasize the point that any aspect of an educational experience that contributes to, or detracts from learning is the legitimate concern of educational evaluation. Evaluation can, and should take place at different levels of specificity. At the macroanalytic level evaluation is concerned with an analysis of the value of the curriculum overall. At the microanalytic level individual teachers or supervisors might be concerned with evaluating the success of a single teaching session or a period of observation, practice or reflection in the clinical setting. Between these two extremes lies a range of areas for consideration in any evaluation exercise. A number of these will now be considered as examples of evaluation at different levels of specificity.

In essence the evaluation described in subsequent examples contributes to curriculum evaluation, since the curriculum encapsulates all aspects of any educational programme, but course managers will need to give particular attention to the overall programme. The elements of nursing curricula have been discussed in the previous chapter, but for purposes of illustration here a simple curriculum model is used to develop the evaluation theme. (See Fig. 6.3.)

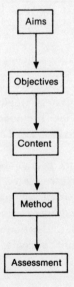

Fig. 6.3 A simple curriculum model

Clearly, in this sequential systems model, the formulation of an evaluation strategy is the last component in the design sequence. In practice of course, curriculum planners consider evaluation and other issues in a more integrated fashion. Nevertheless, the curriculum cannot be evaluated until it is complete.

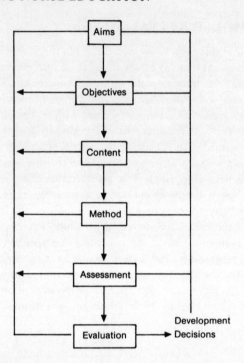

Fig. 6.4   Curriculum evaluation

Bearing in mind the previous discussion regarding the characteristics of evaluation, the purpose of any strategy would be to elicit information on the value of each of the curriculum components and to enable subsequent development and improvements to be made. This is represented diagrammatically in Fig. 6.4.

The model shown in Fig. 6.4 incorporates both the possibility for continuous curriculum monitoring, formative course evaluation developments, and more radical modifications resulting from summative evaluation. Whilst clinical supervisors will undoubtedly contribute to this process and many will serve on course or curriculum committees, this section will not be developed further here since it is primarily the responsibility of course managers.

Evaluation of teaching
The continued competence and professional development of any teacher or clinical supervisor depends greatly on the extent to which she is willing and able to engage in, and make use of, evaluation of her teaching. This requires of teachers a degree of personal and professional maturity sufficient to be tolerant of challenges to competence and self-esteem.

A teacher or supervisor unwilling to scrutinize herself or be subjected to scrutiny by peers or students, will soon develop a self-image based on personal propaganda rather than on realistic feedback. Three methods of evaluation are considered here: self evaluation, peer evaluation, and evaluation by students. A comprehensive review would incorporate all three methods. Firstly, self evaluation, which might usefully focus on continued credibility as a teacher or supervisor. For example, important characteristics of clinical supervisors or mentors is that they act as role models and are both clinically and professionally up to date. Periodic review of these features will provide evaluation information from which individuals can decide whether or not they need to take action to develop or improve. A check-list provides a useful means by which reflection can be focused on key issues. An example of some items that clinical supervisors might employ is shown in Table 6.1.

Table 6.1 Examples of items from a self evaluation check list for clinical supervisors

1. Do I reed the nursing press and discuss current professional issues with colleagues?
2. Am I up to date with publications and developments in my specialist field?
3. Do I attend continuing education events of both a general and specialist nature?
4. Do I make full use of professional library resources?
5. Have I visited other centres specializing in my branch of nursing?
6. Do I have a personal philosophy for nursing care delivery?
7. Is my philosophy consistent with current expectations for nursing practice?
8. Is my philosophy evident in my practice?
9. Do I have a commitment to developing junior colleagues?
10. Do I adequately assess their learning needs?
    (These items are by no means an exhaustive list)

A useful exercise would be to consider the role of the clinical supervisor with colleagues, and to formulate a list of items against which current supervisory practice could be evaluated. The importance of self evaluation, like other forms of evaluation, is limited if no action culminates from the information collected. But the difficulties of being objective and of accepting both strengths and weaknesses equally should not be underestimated. The subject of self evaluation is discussed and explored in more detail by Kilty (1978) but it should be stressed that there is no substitute for experiential learning where self concept is concerned. Only when readers begin to consider the criteria against which they can judge their own performance will they begin to engage in meaningful self evaluation.

Peer evaluation has a number of advantages over self-evaluation given that most of us find it difficult to be truly objective. We tend to employ various ego defence mechanisms to limit damage to self esteem. Rowntree cites research that indicates that we may tend to be more realistic in our expectations of our peers than of our own work (Rowntree, 1977). The idea of reviewing practice with a colleague, whether it be nursing or teaching practice, is a truly professional ideal and provides a very suitable mechanism for the maintenance of standards. The alternation of roles also provides teachers and clinical supervisors with experience in facilitating and encouraging reflection, evaluation and action planning, a process of central importance in facilitating student learning. Peer evaluation may take the form of facilitated self review, or observation and feedback on supervisory performance from a colleague. Thus, the type of check-list described above (see Table 6.1) and the methods to be considered under student evaluation can both be employed to good effect.

Student evaluation of teaching and learning experiences is probably the most

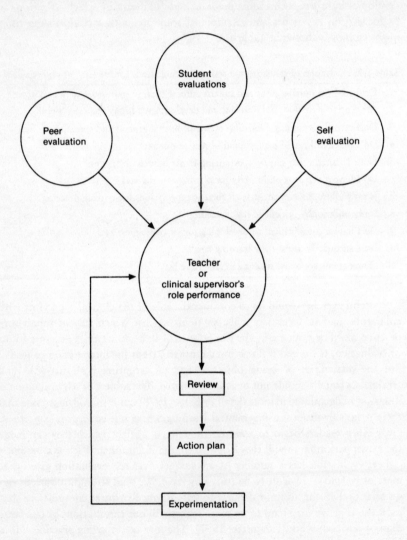

Fig. 6.5 An evaluation process

commonly employed evaluation method. Useful questionnaires for evaluating more formal teaching sessions can be found in the ENB's *Post Basic Clinical Studies Course Evaluation Package* (ENB, undated). Perhaps more difficult is the evaluation of clinically-based learning experiences. If learning experiences are negotiated and clinical placements discussed with students by supervisors at the outset, it is likely that the experience will be well structured with general objectives and learning opportunities made explicit.

Evaluation can then be focused on specific aspects of the teaching-learning process. Although students might be regarded as the most important source of evaluation information, teachers and supervisors should be aware of some potential problems. Students' evaluations may, in some circumstances, reflect more accurately their own learning difficulties, and relate less to the style and expertise of the teacher or supervisor than is apparently the case. For this reason, radical remedial action in response to feedback from one or two students may be misguided. Like all evaluative information, the most valid is likely to be that which can be identified as a consistent trend. When many students consistently report negatively on an aspect of teaching or supervisory performance further reflection and action are legitimate. These three elements of evaluation of teaching or supervisory performance serve as the first stage in a process of improvement and are outlined in Fig. 6.5.

The teacher or supervisor next needs time to review and reflect on the evaluations available. Time to reflect cannot be stressed too greatly and is often lacking in many aspects of nursing practice. During this period consideration can be given to the validity and reliability (concepts discussed later in this chapter) of evaluations, to their relative priority for responsive action, and to the facilitating and inhibiting influences which have contributed to the areas under review. From this will emerge an agenda for action. The action plan, which may be unwritten and unverbalized, or negotiated with a colleague in peer review, should specify areas for development in terms of behaviours or attitudes which can be experimented with in subsequent teaching or supervisory activities. These new approaches or activities will then become the subject of further review in a continual process of professional development.

Evaluating clinical areas

The significance of the clinical environment in nurse education cannot be underestimated. It provides the most substantial part of most programmes and serves to create many of the most important opportunities for learning. It might be argued that in the past there existed an implicit assumption that allocations to clinical areas were premised on the idea of learning by osmosis. By placing students in a work setting with highly skilled practitioners skills would flow down a gradient from the qualified practitioner to the student until an equality in competence was achieved. Clearly, something of this nature may well have occurred in some clinical areas, but it most definitely did not in others.

More recently researchers have investigated the factors that influence learning during clinical allocations (Fretwell, 1982; Orton, 1981; Ogier, 1982). They have been successful in identifying factors which should now be considered when evaluating proposed or utilized clinical experience. Readers may well have participated in, or been the subject of clinical profiles or audits.

Profiling clinical areas

Most Schools of Nursing in England have now developed their own systems for evaluating, approving and monitoring clinical areas for nurse education programmes. The factors considered and the review mechanisms and techniques employed will vary but these themes are likely to be common to all:

1. The experience available, (patient numbers, type, turnover etc.)
2. The organization of nursing care delivery, (the use of nursing model(s); planned, systematic care; individual/team approaches; communication systems etc.)
3. The learning climate, (identification and utilization of learning opportunities; the quality of staff relationships; the extent to which supervision is planned and organized; the level and commitment of supervision)

The evaluation is likely to involve contributions from clinical supervisors in the area under review, service nurses and tutorial staff. Interview, observation, discussion, reviews of documentation and statistical methods are often employed to generate the evaluation information required (see the next section).

An example of a pro forma which serves as guidance in this process is shown as Table 6.2. The evaluation of clinical areas should not be perceived as an inspection by the hierarchy but as an opportunity for tutorial and service colleagues to negotiate and plan the most effective use of the learning opportunities available. Many clinical supervisors will have already considered most of the areas identified in Table 6.2, but some readers may value the opportunity to review the clinical area for which they are responsible as a further dimension of self evaluation. Reflecting on these items with one's colleagues in the ward or unit may serve well as a means of identifying additional continuing education needs for oneself or one's colleagues.

METHODS OF EVALUATION

A number of methods are available to collect evaluation information, and these broadly fall into one of two categories. They are either quantitative in nature, that is to say the information elicited can be analysed numerically and is therefore open to statistical analysis, or qualitative, which will elicit a richness of experiences and processes not captured by quantitative measures. Each will now be considered in turn.

Table 6.2   Dorset School of Nursing Profile of Clinical Area

WARD/DEPT._____
1. What are the main aims of the service which your ward/dept. provides?

Patients
2. Briefly describe the client/patient population:
   Numbers:
   Age range:
   Dependency:
   Length of stay:

Physical environment
3. (a)   What factors contribute positively to the care of patients?

   (b)   What factors detract from the care offered to patients?

Establishments
4. Describe the numbers and grades of nursing staff available:
   On day duty:
   Night duty:
   Community nurse attachement:

5. Give details of the further professional development of all trained staff since qualification.

6. What other staff participate in the care offered to patients? (e.g. O.T., doctors and any others).

7. Briefly describe their involvement:

Clinical communication
8. How is the continuity of care organized:
   Are there clearly defined written ward aims/policies available to all staff?

9. What form do the Handover Reports take?

10. What staff are involved?

11. Describe the staff meetings that are held. Their purpose and the staff in attendance.

12. Do all patients have an up-to-date care plan?

13. Describe any problems which you are experiencing in using a nursing process.

14. How is the nursing staff organized to deliver care?

15. How far ahead is the off duty planned?

Therapeutic programme
16. What activities take place in your ward/dept. which are part of the patients' treatment?
    Prescribe activities (e.g. group therapy, physical treatments, occupation etc.)

    Unplanned activities (e.g. spontaneous social activity)

17. How do you enable patients to exercise choice in their day-to-day activities?

Table 6.2 *cont.*

The learning environment

18. What opportunities for learning does your ward/dept. offer student nurses?

19. What in your opinion is the maximum number of students who can fully benefit from the experience you offer?

20. Could your ward offer experiences to:
    1st year students   Yes/No
    2nd year students   Yes/No
    3rd year students   Yes/No

21. What do you enjoy most about having learners in your ward?

22. Do you find any difficulties associated with having learners in your ward? Please specify.

23. Whose responsibility is the teaching of learners in your ward?

24. In what ways do you enable students to learn?

25. Is there a planned programme of teaching?

26. Are there clear learning objectives and how are they used?

27. What support would you like from the tutorial staff in meeting your teaching responsibility?

28. Name the assessors in your ward/dept.

29. What help would you like in order to develop your teaching skills?

30. What opportunities are there for students to participate in ward rounds, case conferences, etc.?

31. What opportunities are there for students to be involved in the management of your ward/dept?

32. In what other ways do you prepare the student to take responsibility?

Evaluation

33. Who is responsible for completing the students' ward reports?

34. How are students involved in completing their ward reports?

35. What difficulties do you encounter in evaluating students' progress?

Quantitative methods

The key feature of evaluation instruments used to produce quantitative information is that they employ some form of rating scale which enables, at the minimum, numerical summation (as shown in Fig. 6.6) and often more elaborate statistical analysis.

Leaving aside the validity of the example in Fig. 6.6 it illustrates the 'closed' response demanded from students, who can do no more than comply with the

Place a tick in the box that most closely corresponds to your opinion

The sessions were:

	Very useful	Useful	Not useful
Session X			
Session Y			

Fig. 6.6 Items from an evaluation questionnaire permitting numerical summation

requirements dictated by the framework of the questionnaire by placing a tick in the box which most closely corresponds with their opinion. The advantage, of course, is that the resulting evaluation information is easily handled and can be summated to give an overall picture of students' evaluations of particular sessions. It would, therefore, be possible to say, for example, that 70 per cent of respondents valued session X as 'very useful', and 20 per cent as 'useful' and 10 per cent as 'not useful'.

Quantitative approaches are evident in many questionnaires, attitude scales, observation schedules, interaction analyses and other forms of rating scale. One of the most commonly employed methods is the questionnaire and consideration will now be given to this method as an example of the strengths and weaknesses of quantitative techniques.

The questionnaire method can be used to survey the opinions and perceptions of students undergoing some educational experience. A survey is defined by Oppenheim (1968) as 'a form of planned collection of data for the purpose of description, or prediction as a guide to action' and is, therefore, ideally suited to the purpose of evaluation. The first consideration in any survey is the sampling of the population to be surveyed. This need not concern us since in virtually all circumstances in educational evaluation the whole population, that is all the students on the course, is invited to complete the questionnaire. Our primary concern then is with the design of the questionnaire.

The fundamental consideration is that it should be both valid and reliable. That is to say it should be designed in such a way as to elicit information relating to the issue under review, and be structured in such a way as to encourage a common understanding among respondents as to the meaning and requirements of each item. In order to determine this, the questionnaire may have to be piloted and subsequently refined. Using a similar group of students in a placement for which the questionnaire is designed, the clinical supervisor could determine whether or not the students' understanding of the questions or items was as had

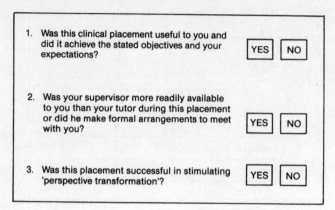

1. Was this clinical placement useful to you and did it achieve the stated objectives and your expectations?   YES   NO

2. Was your supervisor more readily available to you than your tutor during this placement or did he make formal arrangements to meet with you?   YES   NO

3. Was this placement successful in stimulating 'perspective transformation'?   YES   NO

Fig. 6.7 Examples of unsatisfactory items from evaluation questionnaires

been intended. Surprisingly, for many questionnaire designers, this is not always the case with the first draft. Ambiguity often prevails over clarity, and only becomes evident to the evaluator on usage.

Common pitfalls include putting too many elements into each item, poor grammar and the use of jargon. Figure 6.7 shows some examples of unsatisfactory items.

Various scaling and item construction methods are available, some of which are shown in Fig. 6.8.

Notice that in the examples given using a multiple item scale no column is provided for a neutral or 'don't know' response. This type of Likert forced decision scale reduces the possibility of unhelpful 'don't know' responses or the 'central tendency error' of opting for the neutral column. The examples shown are all closed questions forcing a specific response. A semi-open questionnaire item might employ the method of sentence completion. This has the advantage of ensuring the student responds to the focus of concern but permits an expression of opinion not possible with closed items (See Fig. 6.9 for an example). In order to permit free comment closed questionnaire items often include a comments section following each item or group of items.

Having considered briefly here some of the considerations important to questionnaire design, readers might wish to develop their skills further in this area, and should consult the references at the end of this chapter. When a valid and reliable evaluation instrument has been developed the possibilities for analysis extend from simple summation to complex statistical analysis, although this may rarely be required to enable informed decision. Criticisms of the quantitative approach are that it is restrictive and therefore may deny exposure of important evaluation issues, and is teacher-led and therefore more likely to be biased. These problems are said to be lessened by the use of qualitative methods.

- My clinical supervisor was available
  for consultation when required.   Agree   Disagree

- Was your clinical supervisor available
  for consultation when you required her?   YES   NO

- Would you say your clinical supervisor was:

    ALWAYS   ☐

    OFTEN   ☐

    RARELY   ☐

    or NEVER   ☐

    available for consultation when required?

	Strongly Agree	Agree	Disagree	Disagree Strongly
* Clinical Supervisors should be up-to-date with clinical practice.				

- Indicate how important you think it
  is for clinical facilitators to be:

	Very Important	Important	Not Important	Undesirable
(a) up-to-date with clinical practice				
(b) approachable				
(c) perceptive				
(d) honest				
(e) demanding				
(f) co-operative				

- By placing a number from 1–6 in the boxes against the following list of attributes, please indicate your opinion as to which you regard as most important. Number 1 indicates the most important and number 6 the least. No number can be used more than once.

    Clinical supervisors should be:

    up-to-date with clinical practice   ☐
    approachable   ☐
    perceptive   ☐
    honest   ☐
    demanding   ☐
    co-operative   ☐

Fig. 6.8 Examples of different ways of posing evaluation questionnaire items

In your own words, complete the following sentence
to express your views regarding:

(a) The qualities most important in Clinical
     Supervisors are. . . . .
. . . .
. . . .
. . . .

Fig. 6.9 An example of semi-open evaluation questionnaire

Qualitative methods

The main purpose of these methods is to illuminate educational experiences in a more comprehensive sense, yielding 'richer' information. Their main disadvantage is that the information is hard to collate and can not easily be summated for easy reference. Nevertheless, the more student-centred nurse education becomes (see Chapter Three), the more appropriate will qualitative evaluation become.

Qualitative evaluation employs a range of methods in a flexible fashion in order to achieve a complete picture of the educational experience. Interviews with students (both structured and unstructured), discussion, participant and non-participant observation, diaries, self-reporting and critical incident techniques are all appropriate methods. Gale and O'Pray (1981) have made the point that qualitative evaluation need not be entirely open-ended nor without structure and many evaluation strategies combine both quantitative and qualitative instruments.

The clinical supervisor is ideally placed to adopt the role of participant observer in clinical learning experiences, and to engage with the student in interactive qualitative evaluation. A qualitative approach should not, however, be an excuse to ignore the key characteristics of the evaluation process detailed earlier in this chapter.

Perhaps the major problem confronting teachers and supervisors is the potential volume of qualitative information and the subsequent difficulties of analysis. The value and richness of student-initiated and student-focused evaluation, generated from interview or group discussion situations, should however, override any reluctance to record and utilize qualitative information.

It is likely that most course managers, teachers and clinical supervisors will employ an eclectic approach to evaluation and use both quantitative and qualitative methods. Formative evaluation is perhaps more likely to attract the open-ended qualitative evaluation discussion, whereas the demands of course or clinical placement closure might dictate an emphasis on quantitative methods. A method used sucessfully, as an adjunct to other evaluation techniques, in the Dorset School's Teaching and Assessing course (ENB 998) is outlined in Fig. 6.10.

1. Individual students brainstorm areas of satisfaction and dissatisfaction with the course.
2. Individuals get together in small groups and compare and collate areas of satisfaction and dissatisfaction.
3. The group converts all areas identified into positive statements. For example: 'I wasn't very happy with the amount of jargon in presentations', becomes 'Presentations were free of jargon'.
4. Each statement is then transferred to a box card and then each box card attached to a large piece of paper against a scale agreed by consensus. For example:

	Strongly Agree	Agree	Disagree	Disagree Strongly
CARDS				

5. The papers are then mounted on the wall, and the whole group will circulate, and each enter a tick in the column which most closely corresponds with their opinion.
6. Finally, the scores are summated to give an overall impression of areas of satisfaction and dissatisfaction within the group. This can then be pursued further in discussion if agreed.

Fig. 6.10 Student-centred evaluation method

This method has the advantage of being student-centred, and often focuses on aspects of course structure and process which would not have been identified in teacher-generated evaluation.

The procedures elaborated in Fig. 6.10 can easily be modified for use with smaller groups in clinical settings. The important points to incorporate in any modified version should be anonymity for student-generated items and an acceptance that the areas identified are important to them and therefore worthy of consideration.

Roles and responsibilities

Evaluation of learning experiences in nurse education involves to a greater or lesser extent all those involved in the programme. However, the responsibility for organizing, initiating and responding to evaluation information is the particular concern of the following individuals or groups.

The course committee

Basic and post-basic nurse education programmes are normally devised by a planning team comprising teachers, clinical specialists, service managers, other significant potential contributors and students. The responsibility of the planning team is to devise a course to meet the requirements of the approving National

Board or validating body and to prepare a course submission to be presented for consideration and approval. Once approved, the management and continued monitoring of a course becomes the responsibility of either a course committee, curriculum development group or some other representative group of contributors to the programme, who can monitor progress and effect change and development

---

Table 6.3 Dorset School of Nursing professional development team course reports

Each course tutor is responsible for preparing a terminal course report (or interim reports as required) for consideration by the course committee. Each course committee is charged with the following responsibilities.

1. Ensuring that the course operates within the specification defined by the English National Board.
2. Monitoring learning outcomes and considering course evaluation, reporting to the Director of Nurse Education on all aspects of the curriculum.
3. Considering suggestions put forward by the teaching team, the staff in placement settings, students and others, on any aspect of the course.
4. Reporting to the Director on the initiation and control of amendments to the presentation of the course.

(It is acknowledged that, in practice, minor modifications resulting from evaluation will be initiated by the course tutor and reported to the course committee.)

To assist the course committee in its deliberations reports should be formulated to include information covering at least the following areas.

1. Title of course
2. Course number (where appropriate), and intake number under current approval
3. Starting date
4. Completion date
5. Number of students course approved for
6. Number of enquiries
7. Number of applications received
8. Number interviewed
9. Number offered places
10. Number commenced
11. Number completed
12. Number discontinued (D)
    withdrawn   (W)
13. Course evaluation report citing strengths and weaknesses in structure, process and outcome. Consideration should be given to all aspects of the course curriculum, its implementation and outcome. Clinical placements and visits should be reported. Examination, assessment or student profiles should be reviewed and relevant data reported. Resource usage should be reviewed. A summary of the main points from student evaluations should be itemized.
14. Conclusions
    A brief resumé of the strengths and weaknesses of the course should include a list of items or areas to be considered more specifically by the course committee.

in response to course evaluation. A course committee normally reports to the Director of Nurse Education (or head of the institution) who is responsible to the National Board for the overall running of the school or institution.

The course committee will be empowered to make revisions in the presentation of the course within the regulations laid down by the National Board or approving authority.

Course tutors

Course tutors are more specifically responsible for implementing the evaluation strategy devised by the course planning team and for collating evaluation information and presenting it to the course committee for consideration. An example of a pro forma used for post-basic courses is shown in Table 6.3 illustrating the information which is submitted to the course committee.

Clinical supervisors

Clinical Supervisors will have developed methods of evaluating learning experiences in their area, and may initiate modification to opportunities available for learning. It is equally important that supervisors feed information to the course tutor, or through representatives to ensure that as broad a picture as possible is built up. In this way feedback on all aspects of a nurse education programme can be considered by a course committee and decisions regarding developments recorded in the minutes.

This is especially important in order to be able to demonstrate to an education officer from the validating and approving body how the programme has been reviewed and developed over time.

Making decisions

It is important that evaluation is not seen as a ritualistic exercise with no substantive outcome. The only purpose for initiating the process described in this chapter is to develop and enhance learning experiences. An evaluation strategy must incorporate mechanisms for ensuring that agreed information can be acted upon. This may involve negotiation with many others involved in the programme, and not unusaully, a change in attitudes or priorities. But the greatest disservice to sudents is done by working through an evaluation exercise with little or no intention or possibility of effecting change.

Recommendations or proposed action to achieve development or change is most likely to be effected if a logical sequence is followed. The problem-solving cycle most familiar to readers in the form of the nursing process serves well as a protocol for action. Discussion in this chapter has related particularly to the diagnostic or assessment phase of the cycle. A plan of action should follow detailing how, where and when modifications will be made.

In implementing proposed developments, evaluators will need to be aware of possible constraining factors and resistance to changes which accompany any innovation or threat to the status quo. Finally, evaluation of the changes implemented should complete the cycle and indicates the centrality of evaluation to the process of teaching and learning, just as in nursing practice.

CONCLUSION

This chapter has considered and reviewed the key characteristics of evaluation of nurse education programmes. The elements discussed can be brought together as a model and are shown in Fig. 6.11.

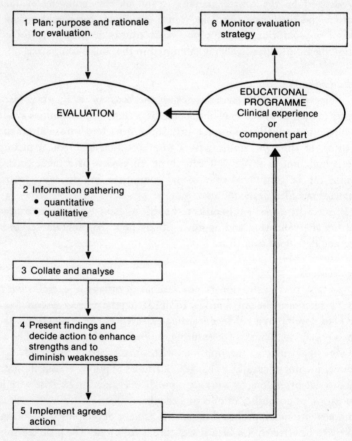

Fig. 6.11 An evaluation model

Coles and Gale-Grant (1985) identify a series of questions that might be posed in seeking to evaluate the evaluation. They provide a useful statement on which to close this chapter.

Is the evaluation meeting its requirements?
Has it adopted appropriate methodologies?
Has it accounted for its findings in appropriate ways?
Has it reported its findings clearly and concisely?
Has it stimulated decision making and development?

Implementation of the process outlined in this chapter should achieve all of these goals.

REFERENCES

Coles, C. R. and Gale-Grant, J. (1985). *Curriculum Evaluation in Medical and Health Care Evaluation.* Medical Education Research Booklet, No 1. Dundee: Association for the Study of Medical Education.

English National Board for Nursing, Midwifery and Health Visiting (undated). *Post Basic Clinical Studies Course Evaluation Package.* London: ENB.

English National Board for Nursing, Midwifery and Health Visiting. (1987). *Course Approval Process; rules, regulations and guidelines.* (1987/28/MAT), London, ENB.

Easterbury-Smith, M. and Tanton, M. (1985). 'Turning course evaluation from an end to a means', *Personnel Management.* April 1985, pages 15–7.

Fretwell, J. E. (1982). *Ward Teaching and Learning: Sister and the Learning Environment.* London: Royal College of Nursing.

Gale, J. and O'Pray, M. (1981). 'The development and implications of frames of reference in curriculum evaluation programmes: the experience of a British School of Medicine', *British Journal of Educational Technology,* 1, pages 49–63.

Kilty, J. (1978). *Self and Peer Assessment.* Surrey University, Human Potential Research Project.

Oppenheim, A. N. (1968). *Questionnaire Design and Attitude Measurement.* London: Heinemann.

Ogier, M. (1982). *An Ideal Sister?: a study of the leadership style and verbal interactions of ward sisters with nurse learners in general hospitals.* London: Royal College of Nursing.

Orton, H. (1981). *Ward Learning Climate: a study of the role of the ward sister in relation to student nurse learning on the ward.* London: Royal College of Nursing.

Rowntree, D. (1977). *Assessing Students: How Shall We Know Them?* London: Harper and Row.

CHAPTER SEVEN

STUDY SKILLS AND LEARNING STYLES

INTRODUCTION

Learning is a lifelong process, it may be planned or unplanned, conscious or unconscious. Most individuals are unaware of how learning takes place although some identify that they learn better by one way than another. This may be indicated by comments such as 'I need to do it so that I can understand' or 'I need time to think about that'. In this way the individual is expressing the conditions she requires to learn well.

The psychology of learning is included in the curriculum for those on formal teacher preparation courses, and therefore it may be assumed that qualified teachers have an awareness of factors that may affect an individual's progress. Student nurses however are taught by many teachers, both qualified and unqualified, and this latter group especially may not have had an opportunity to study the theory of learning. In Chapter Three the theory of educating adults was discussed, in this chapter the focus of facilitating learning through developing study skills and individual learning styles will be based upon the experiential learning theory described by Kolb (1975). Understanding how learning takes place enables appropriate learning strategies to be selected, forms a basis of study skills and is likely to result in more effective learning.

A gap may exist between what is learnt in theory and what happens in practice. Teaching methods, in both the classroom and clinical environments are likely to relate more to tradition, fashion and individual ability rather that what is appropriate to the needs of the learner. It may be argued that a better knowledge of learning theory is likely to lead to more effective identification of learning needs and in turn more effective teaching to meet these needs.

THEORIES

Kolb's experiential learning theory

Kolb has described a model of experiential learning (Fig. 7.1) which suggests that learning, change and growth are facilitated by an integrated process. This model describes a learning cycle consisting of four phases which are dynamic. The cycle commences with the phase of concrete experience, this may be described as 'here and now' experiences during which learning takes place by actual involvement. This is followed by a phase of reflective observation in which 'thinking over' the concrete experience results in an increase in learning as the individual becomes aware of more information and is able to make sense of it. The third phase is abstract conceptualization in which analysis of the learning experience leads to the formation of conclusions or concepts. A concept may be defined as:

> A general notion of things or events arrived at by processes of perceptual classification and discrimination, used as a basis for thought and expressed through symbolic language.
>
> International Dictionary of Education

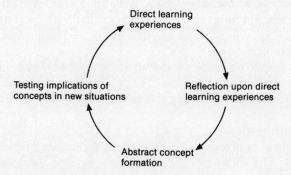

Fig. 7.1 Experiential learning cycle: after Kolb (1975)

The concepts formed can be used to modify existing behaviour or to help select new experiences which form the fourth phase, active experimentation, of the cycle. In this final phase the concepts are tested in new situations, providing further concrete experience which starts the cycle again. Kolb argues that as the individual develops he learns by all these phases, but is likely to develop a preference for learning more by one method than another and thus a preferred learning style is developed. Kolb describes similarities between his model and Piaget's (1984) model of cognitive development.

Piaget's model of cognitive development

Piaget described four main stages of development which he associated with maturity, identifying approximate ages at which children reach each stage. These stages are:

1. *Sensori-motor*: from birth to eighteen months.
2. *Pre-operational*: from eighteen months to seven years.

3. *Concrete operational*: from seven years to eleven years.
4. *Formal operational*: from eleven years to adulthood.

Stage 1. Sensori-motor

In this stage the child learns to identify information it is receiving through its senses, whilst at the same time developing co-ordination. Awareness develops of the outside world and of the fact that objects and people continue to exist even when out of sight. The game of peek-a-boo played with the child's favourite toy may be used to illustrate this; by eighteen months of age the child will realise where the toy is when hidden behind another object and will attempt to reach it.

Stage 2. Pre-operational

In this stage simple, very generalized concepts may be formed e.g. all men are daddy, all four-legged animals are dogs. As the child develops discrimination gradually increases, but there remains an inability to deal with the abstract.

Stage 3. Concrete operational

During this stage the beginning of abstract thinking is developed, but Piaget suggests this only relates to 'real' things. The child cannot yet cope with abstract concepts or symbols. Problem-solving is therefore possible but limited.

Stage 4. Formal operational

In this stage the ability to reason scientifically develops, enabling problem-solving using symbols. The ability to form hypotheses and test them out is also developed.

Learning styles

Individual learning style is shaped by natural learning experiences that occur through maturation. Kolb states that:

> As a result of our hereditary equipment, or particular past life experiences and the demands of our present environment, people develop learning styles that emphasise some learning abilities over others.

He suggests that each of us develops a unique style with particular strengths and weaknesses. Using a self-descriptive inventory these strengths and weaknesses were tested resulting in the identification of four learning styles. Each style combines the poles of two independent dimensions, Abstract – Concrete and Active – Reflective (Fig. 7.2).

Laschinger and Boss (1984) have described the characteristics of the four identified learning styles as follows:

1. *Diverger*. Predominantly concrete experience and reflective observation. Their greatest strength lies in their imaginative ability. They are interested in people and tend to be emotional.

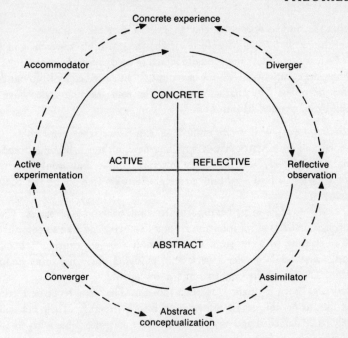

Fig. 7.2 Model of individual learning styles: after Kolb (1975)

2. *Assimilator.* Predominantly reflective observation and abstract conceptualization. Their greatest strength lies in creating theoretical models. They are less interested in people, more concerned with the practical use of ideas.
3. *Converger.* Predominantly abstract conceptualization and active experimentation. Their greatest strength lies in the application of ideas. They are relatively unemotional, preferring things to people.
4. *Accommodator.* Predominantly active experimentation and concrete experience. Their greatest strength lies in doing things. They tend to solve problems in an intuitive 'trial and error' manner and are 'risk-takers' who rely heavily on other people for information rather than use their own analytical ability.

Learning styles are unlikely to be permanently fixed but will alter in relation to motivation and circumstances. When following a course of planned study the students are unlikely to be able to influence the teaching method and therefore need to be able to learn from all the experiences offered whether they match their individual learning styles or not. It is however likely that the students will apply for courses which offer the type of experience that will suit their individual learning styles. Kolb suggests that 'each discipline attracts individuals with a learning style congruent with its structure of knowledge' and also that 'learning style is further accentuated through education and experience in the discipline'. Should there be incongruence between learning style and learning experiences it is likely that the student will either change style or leave the course.

Peter Honey and Alan Mumford (1986) using Kolb's research as a basis, designed a learning styles questionnaire which related to four learning styles (Fig. 7.3). These are compatible with the two dimensions described by Kolb but do not combine the poles. The characteristics of the four learning styles have been described by Honey and Mumford as:

1. *Activists.* Learn well from immediate experience, they tend to be open-minded and enthusiastic about anything new, although become bored with longer term consolidation. They often act first and think afterwards. Problems are solved by brainstorming. Activists like to be the centre of activity.

2. *Reflectors.* Learn best by having time to think back on experiences. They are thorough, collecting information from all sources, and like to complete this before coming to a decision. On the whole they are cautious, thoughtful people who tend to take a back seat, enjoying observing other people in action. They naturally tend to adopt a low profile.

3. *Theorists.* Learn by logical, abstract thought. They tend to be perfectionists and like to be able to fit information into a structure. Their behaviour is likely to be detached and analytical, they feel uncomfortable with emotional and subjective judgments.

4. *Pragmatists.* Learn by trying out new ideas to see if they work. They will take every opportunity to experiment, usually they are full of ideas and like to get on with things quickly. Their nature is likely to be impatient, they enjoy challenges and are essentially down to earth practical people who enjoy problem solving.

Whilst Kolb and Honey and Mumford have described different learning styles there are similarities to be found between them. The basic experiential theory does not alter, only the method of identifying the learning style and its name. All agree that individuals develop specific learning styles as a result of their life experiences and that these styles may affect their ability to learn from new experiences.

LEARNING STYLES

Individual learning styles related to nurse education

The relevance of individual learning style to learning to nurse may be identified as follows:

1. Recognizing that nursing students will have developed an individual learning style prior to commencing nurse training.
2. Understanding that the learning experiences offered in nursing courses may not be congruent with the student's individual learning style.

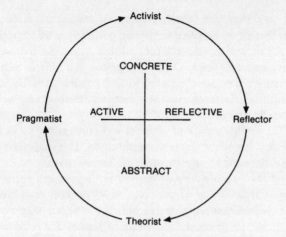

Fig. 7.3 Individual learning styles: after Honey and Mumford (1975)

3. Realizing that the students have the potential to alter their learning styles in order to enable them to benefit from the learning experiences which are offered.

The study by Honey and Mumford is of particular use to teachers of nurses in that it suggests strategies that may be used for developing non-dominant styles. This is achieved by selecting an area in which the student feels it would be beneficial to develop her learning style. It is necessary to analyse her responses to the questions that relate to that particular style, and to identify inappropriate responses which the student feels could be altered. Strategies may then be planned to develop this area. For example, should the student answer yes to the statement 'On balance I talk more than I listen' then plans may be made to develop her listening skills. If desired the student could attempt to develop an all-round ability which will enable her to learn effectively from all types of learning experiences.

Research on individual learning styles relevant to nurse education

Laschinger (1984) in her study found that the majority of entrants to nursing had concrete learning styles and were more influenced by people-orientated factors in career choices than those with abstract styles. A later study by Laschinger (1986) suggested that nursing environments were predominantly concrete in learning orientation. These studies would appear to support Kolb's theory that individuals are attracted to courses that provide learning experiences compatible with their learning styles.

Ostmoe et al. (1984) tested two groups of baccalaureate nursing students for their learning strategies preferences. One group was commencing its first course of nursing and the second group was completing its last course. Using a questionnaire they identified usually-preferred strategies and seldom-preferred strategies. The first group appeared to respond positively to all strategies whereas the second group showed a preference for traditional strategies that were teacher-centred, passive and organized. Ostmoe suggested that this is because of the learning experiences they were exposed to and possible negative attitudes of others. The ability of the teacher to use a particular method may well affect its acceptability to the student.

Gosby (1987) studied groups of students and pupil nurses to determine the effect of individual learning styles in nurse education. This study used Honey and Mumford's questionnaire to identify preferred learning styles.

It was found that the majority of learners in training had either activist or reflector learning styles, being 37 per cent and 45 per cent respectively. It was found that the predominant reflector style of first year nurses (60 per cent) altered throughout training to an equal distribution of activist and reflector styles for third year nurses (44 per cent each). It would appear that the learning experiences offered resulted in some students altering their preferred learning style. When comparing student and pupil nurses it was found that pupils were more likely to have an activist learning style by the end of their course (80 per cent) which may reflect the more practical nature of this training and therefore the different emphasis in learning experiences.

The group was also tested to determine whether preferred teaching strategies could be identified and whether there was a relationship between these strategies and individual learning styles. Overall there was a preference for the teaching methods of demonstration (88 per cent), video (80 per cent), film (78 per cent), and discussion (77 per cent), with least preferred methods being role play (18 per cent), programmed learning (39 per cent) and games (45 per cent). It appeared that in general, nursing students liked to be taught by a variety of methods. It was surprising to finu ine high scores for films and videos which are essentially passive methods of learning. This may be explained by the fact that being visual they offer concrete experience and also that they reflect 'natural' learning methods. As television is an everyday fixture it may be suggested that students are acclimatized to learning from documentaries and similar educational programmes. The lecture score of 56 per cent indicated it to be a fairly well-accepted method. It is of course a familiar method and one to which students have been socialized prior to entering nursing. The dislike of role play may reflect upon the skills of the teachers using this method or alternatively the students' inexperience and unfamiliarity with this method. Psychological learning theory and trends in teaching favour active teaching methods but not all teachers are adequately prepared to use such methods.

Identifying learning opportunities to suit learning styles

The theory of learning styles suggests that different learning strategies suit different learning styles. This does not mean that students will only learn from strategies that match their individual learning style, but that they are likely to learn best from these strategies and may require more help where the strategy does not suit their learning style. The theory does provide an explanation as to why some students learn more effectively than others given the same learning conditions. Pask and Scott (1972) found that learning was better when students and teaching method were matched. However, Green (1974) on testing nursing students concluded that:

> To group together students with similar learning preferences and attendant teaching method could be restrictive rather than helpful to the development of effective learning, especially if it were to be the predominant approach in a curriculum.

In order to become a qualified nurse students are expected to learn from a range of learning strategies in both the clinical and classroom environments. In Chapter Four it was identified that learning skills can be divided into three categories.

1. *Psycho-motor skills*: related to practice.
2. *Cognitive skills*: related to knowledge.
3. *Affective skills*: related to attitudes.

Psycho-motor learning skills

This category encompasses the practical skills involved in nursing. Whilst these skills require a knowledge base they are easily learnt through the strategies of demonstration and practice under supervision. Those students who have activist learning styles are likely to learn well by this method. Kolb (1976), cited in Laschinger and Boss (1984), suggested that 'concrete learners learn best in environments which involve direct experience'. Laschinger and Boss (1984) stated as a result of their studies that 'nursing attracts concrete learners more than abstract ones'. They identified a significant increase in concrete learning style amongst advanced students which led them to conclude that 'learning style is accentuated with an increased exposure to the discipline'. Nurse training involves considerable direct experience in the clinical environment which may be reflected in the classroom by use of strategies such as discussion, simulation, role play and other experiential techniques.

Teachers of nurses in either clinical or classroom environments are likely to succeed by selecting active learning strategies. A planned teaching programme in the clinical environment which makes full use of the direct experience available supported by opportunities to analyze and discuss experiences is likely to match the learning styles of the majority of the students, since research would indicate that most are likely to have concrete learning styles. Entrants to nurse training will expect to have direct clinical experience and to learn from it and are likely to have learning styles congruent with the type of course offered or to develop their learning styles in accordance with the experiences offered.

Kitson (1985) suggests that 'the unspoken assumption is that you cannot learn about nursing without doing nursing', an assumption which she suggests is shared by both nurse educators and nurse practitioners. The danger of teaching in the clinical environment is to assume that because a student has done something in practice they know what they are doing. It is important to follow the principles of teaching the following ways:

1. Explaining what is to be learnt.
2. Demonstrating the skill.
3. Allowing the student to ask questions.
4. Providing supervised practice.
5. Questioning the student and reinforcing knowledge.
6. Allowing further practice.
7. Providing feedback on performance.

Once a skilled performance has been achieved and assessment of knowledge is satisfactory the student may be said to be competent. Observing the principles of teaching will produce a 'knowledgeable doer'.

Cognitive skills

A knowledge base is essential for competent nursing practice. Nursing practice based on problem-solving skills requires the possession of academic as well as practical skills. The presentation of knowledge is an influencing factor in the development of cognitive skills. Burnard (1985) states that, 'Many traditional methods offer the students pre-packaged knowledge in indigestible chunks, upon which no reflection takes place.'

Traditional training courses are organized in blocks or modules related to clinical experience. The student is likely to be presented with knowledge related to the clinical speciality as a 'one-off' experience, for example if the paediatric allocation occurs in the first year this is likely to be the only occasion that the student studies the theory of paediatric nursing care. Consequently the final examination at the end of the training course is likely to assess knowledge gained some two years previously. Realistically only a simple reproduction of facts can be expected; higher academic skills of analysis, synthesis and evaluation are unlikely to have been developed to a significant level. Burnard (1985) further suggests that, 'The educated person or educated nurse is the one who has managed to absorb more "facts" than her colleagues.'

Students with abstract learning styles are likely to find it easier to learn the theory of nursing, but when theory is related to practice students with concrete styles will learn equally well. The current assessment scheme is likely to favour those who have the ability to recall knowledge rather than those who although able to apply knowledge find the written examination a 'false' situation and perform less well in these conditions. Continuous assessment schemes would appear to be a more effective method of assessing competence to nurse. In such schemes a variety of assessment methods may be utilized such as learning contracts, project work and research reports. These methods allow for theory and practice to be related and also provide opportunity for academic growth by developing higher level academic skills. The English National Board states that:

All too often student nurses are pairs of hands in the clinical environment and that academically very little progress is made throughout the three years of training.

The need to produce a competent nurse who is knowledgeable about nursing practice and fully able to utilize problem-solving approaches to care is fundamental to the proposals for changing the way in which nurses are educated. This may be achieved by presenting knowledge using experiential teaching strategies which allow the students to discover and develop knowledge themselves. These methods do not need to replace traditional teaching strategies but rather complement them. Burnard (1985) suggests that, 'A combination of traditional and experiential techniques can produce a powerful and comprehensive educational experience.'

He suggests that knowledge can be gained in two ways:

1. Learning through experience.
2. Learning by experience.

In the first way examples may be learning to take blood pressures, bath a patient, feed a patient and other similar practical skills which may be learnt either in the classroom with colleagues or in the clinical environment under the supervison of a nurse teacher or qualified practitioner. The second way involves evaluating direct experience by providing a period of reflection and opportunity to discuss the actual experience in order to clarify what has been learnt. The emphasis of experiential learning is the actual personal experience of the student. Use of experiential theory will benefit students of all individual learning styles.

This theory can be applied by identifying appropriate learning experiences in both classroom and clinical environments which can be taught using experiential strategies. Encouraging the student to use a questioning approach rather than passive acceptance of nursing practice will develop their knowledge base. Learning will be facilitated by allowing the student to discover information for themselves and then helping them to 'make sense' of this information by giving appropriate direction and feedback.

Affective skills

It was identified that individuals with concrete learning styles tended to be more 'people-orientated' than those with abstract styles. One of the most important characteristics in the nurse is her 'caring' attitude although individuals who are too sensitive may find the reality of nursing too difficult to cope with. Margaret Alexander (1983) emphasizes the need for a holistic approach to patient care stating that, 'Learning to nurse is learning to care – learning to care for people, whole people not "parts" of people.' She identifies the need to consider the patient as an individual and respect their different life experiences, problems and accomplishments.

In order to teach the relevant attitudes and values appropriate to nursing it is necessary to create a learning environment in which the students can feel free to explore their own feelings and attitudes towards situations in order to clarify appropriate responses. This may be achieved by the use of experiential methods in the classroom in order to teach interpersonal skills. In the clinical environment the use of role modes and encouragement of students to discuss their experiences and reactions will be helpful. It is important that the students feel that their opinions are of value, and that their responses to situations are recognized as either appropriate or inappropriate rather than being classified as normal or abnormal. In this way development of appropriate nursing attitudes is facilitated.

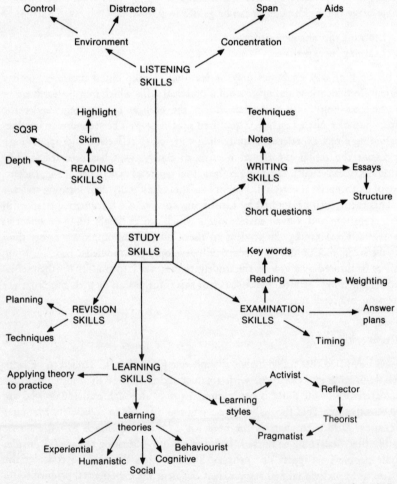

Fig. 7.4 Skills required for effective study: (illustrated as pattern notes: Gosby, 1987)

Study skills

Entrants to nursing will have experience of studying and have developed a level of skills in order to achieve the specified entry qualifications. However since their age range may vary from 17½ to 45 it is likely that some will have had a gap from their most recent study to commencement of training, and therefore that their study skills will have become 'rusty'. Continuing education in nursing also results in qualified nurses needing to renew their study skills in order to follow professional development or higher education courses. Many students who return to studying are anxious about their ability to cope with learning again, especially if the course involves written assessment.

There is a variety of skills necessary for effective study (Fig. 7.4). Each of these is important and there are a variety of techniques available which may improve particular skills.

Reading skills

The ability to cope with the amount of reading required needs to be developed early in a course. There are various techniques that are helpful in developing reading skills. Most students do not think they are able to skim read, although most of us employ this tactic when we pick up the daily paper or read our mail. Often students feel that because the reading is for a formal course it must be important to read every word in case they miss something. The ability to skim read may be improved by use of a highlight pen so that important words or phrases are picked out (providing of course that the book belongs to the student!). A second method which develops reading skills is known as SQ3R as described by Francis Robinson (1970). The formula stands for:

1. *Survey*. The chapter is skimmed to identify whether it appears to be of use. In particular notice is taken of the headings and the final summary.
2. *Question*. Each heading is turned into a question e.g. Study skills becomes: what are study skills? This helps to focus attention on what information is required.
3. *Read*. The section related to the heading is now read to find out the answer to the question formulated.
4. *Recite*. The book is closed and an attempt is made to answer the question in the reader's own words. It may help at this point to jot down cue words. If the question cannot be answered the section is re-read and the stage repeated. The stages of question, read, recite are then repeated for all remaining sections of the chapter.
5. *Review*. Once the chapter has been completed using this technique the book is closed and using the cue words noted as prompts an attempt is made to recall all the information.

Use of techniques such as skimming and SQ3R may increase reading skills resulting in more effective study.

Listening skills

There are various factors that may affect listening skills. These include the noise level in the environment, visual distractions, the behaviour of colleagues, one's own motivation and the voice and delivery of the teacher. This latter factor is particularly important, for example, the speed of delivery, the clarity of speech, the tone of voice and the interest in the subject generated by the teacher.

The control the individual has over the environment is also a relevant factor. If the student is able to control noise levels and other distractions it will be easier to listen. Listening should not be confused with hearing, it is possible to hear what someone says without listening, most of us are capable of making appropriate noises in response to a communication without really taking in what is said. It is necessary to focus one's attention in order to listen well. This may be helped by selecting key words or phrases. Few people can listen and write at the same time therefore it is also necessary to develop good note writing skills so that time is available for listening properly. Preparatory reading for a session may also help in that it will provide a basis of knowledge for linking new information to and in turn increase understanding of what is said.

Writing skills

These include note-writing techniques as well as the ability to write up projects, learning contracts, answer test questions and write extended essays. There are techniques which may be useful in writing notes such as identifying key words, underlining these and using them as headings under which key phrases may be written. It is not a good idea to try to write down every word the teacher says, since this leaves insufficient time for listening and thinking. Good notes should form a basis for further reading and more extensive note-writing in one's own time.

'Sprays' may be used as a quick way of jotting down ideas, these are words or phrases which are 'brain-stormed' and then 'lines' or 'bubbles' used to join relevant words together. This technique may be useful when planning essays or answering examination questions. A development of this method is pattern notes in which one key concept has sprays of related words coming off it. Figure 7.4 is an example of pattern notes. This technique is useful for planning essays, teaching sessions or summarizing reading.

Examination skills

More formal written work such as examination questions requires more specific skills. Effective answering technique relies upon the following:

1. *Reading the question.* It is important to spend time reading the question properly, identifying exactly what is asked. This may be helped by underlining key words. When writing an answer it is useful to read the

question again in between sections in order to ensure one has not strayed from the point.

2. *Planning the answer.* This may be done mentally or on paper depending on what the individual has found to be effective. It is necessary to select appropriate information to answer the question and an answer plan may help to focus attention on the points required. Answer plans should be short and easy to follow.

3. *Identifying the weighting.* The weighting given to each section of the question provides a method of achieving appropriate balance. The highest weighting will indicate the most important information required and the lowest the least important information.

4. *Timing.* It is important to be able to answer the question within the specified time. Questions which are in parts should be timed accordingly. This can be linked by relating to the weighting, e.g. if 40 minutes are available to answer a question and the weighting is 75:25 then the timing would 30:10 minutes.

5. *Reviewing the answer.* It is a good idea to leave a few minutes to re-read one's answer when it is completed. Firstly the question should be re-read and then the answer to determine whether all points asked have been answered.

If all these points are considered and practised then good answering techniques will have been developed. However, this technique is of little use if knowledge has not been learnt well first.

Revision skills

In order to cope effectively with examinations, revision skills need to be developed. It is important for the students to be aware of how they as individuals revise best, becoming aware of factors that influence their ability to revise.

1. Do they learn slowly and need a long revision period, or do they learn best when their stress level is raised a little and therefore do better if they put pressure on themselves?

2. Do they learn best alone or in a study group?

3. Do they learn by rewriting notes or would it be better to record a tape which can be played back?

4. Does doing practice questions help, do they need individual tutorials, do they need a combination of both or do they revise most effectively left to their own devices?

Consideration of all these factors will help to formulate an effective revision plan. Writing a revision plan is useful in identifying what is to be revised, giving those items a priority order and planning how to test oneself to evaluate the effectiveness of one's revison programme. Methods of revision are likely to reflect one's preferred learning strategies.

Learning skills

Most important for effective study is knowledge of how one learns. Awareness of individual learning style will enable selection of appropriate learning strategies. Those with concrete learning styles will learn best by trying to relate theory to practice, writing notes, recording tapes and self-testing. Those with abstract learning styles will learn well by reading around the subject, allowing time for reflection and putting information into a logical structure.

Other essential factors, regardless of learning style, are to be aware of how long a period study can be sustained and also of what time of day studying appears easiest. Generally it is advisable not to study for more than two hours at a time and to plan adequate breaks between period of study to allow knowledge to consolidate. It is important not to feel that the course is controlling the individual but rather that the individual is controlling the course. Time to lead a normal social life with family and friends is vital to maintain one's motivation to continue to study and attain desired objectives. Study plans should allow for natural breaks such as Christmas and also for emergencies to occur such as illness. A plan that is too tightly programmed will result in inability to keep up with the plan should unexpected events occur, with resulting feelings of failure and anxiety. A plan which allows for emergencies will remain attainable and be more likely to succeed.

CONCLUSION

Understanding how one learns is the basis to effective studying. This may be achieved by using the psychological learning theory described by Kolb (1975) which relates to experiential learning. This theory is based on a cycle commencing with direct learning experiences which are followed by reflective thought, the formation of abstract concepts and the testing of these concepts in new situations. Kolb suggests that during development a preference is formed for learning more by one method than another resulting in a preferred learning style.

Kolb *et al.* have researched individual learning styles and suggest that nurses are more likely to have concrete than abstract learning styles. Features of concrete learning styles include the ability to learn well from direct experience and also the likelihood of being more 'people-orientated' than those with abstract styles. Research suggests that nursing offers a concrete learning environment and that entrants to nursing are likely to have learning styles that are congruent to the learning experiences offered.

Awareness of individual learning styles and the underlying experiential theory may enable teachers of nurses to select appropriate learning strategies to facilitate effective learning. It will also provide an explanation of individual learning differences that become apparent among nursing students.

Effective study relies on appropriate development of related study skills such as reading skills, listening skills, writing skills, examination skills, revision skills and learning skills. There are various techniques available that may be utilized to improve these specific skills.

The ability to learn and study effectively is fundamental to the individual's success on any course she chooses to follow. Individual growth and development of academic skills may influence achievement of their full potential. Those involved in teaching nurses may facilitate individual growth by being aware of the theory of learning and applying appropriate techniques to enable personal development.

REFERENCES

Alexander, Margaret F. (1983). *Learning to Nurse*. London: Churchill Livingstone.
Burnard, Philip (1986). *Learning Human Skills – A Guide for Nurses*. London: Heinemann Nursing.
English National Board for Nursing, Midwifery and Health Visiting (1985). *Professional Education/Training Courses*. (Consultation Paper). London: English National Board for Nursing, Midwifery and Health Visiting.
Gosby, Janice (1987). *Individual Learning Styles as a Factor Affecting Nursing Curricula*. MAEd Dissertation, University of Southampton.
Green J. L. (1974). *The Relationship Between Membership in a Curricular Preference Typology and Selected Performance Outcomes*. PhD Thesis, University of California.
Honey, Peter, and Mumford, Alan (1986). *Manual of Learning Styles*. Berkshire: Honey and Mumford.
Kitson, Alison (1985). 'Educating for quality'. *Senior Nurse*, Vol. 3, No. 4, pages 11–16.
Kolb, David, and Fry, Ronald (1975). 'Towards an applied theory of experiential learning', in Cooper, Gary (ed.), *Theories of Group Processes*. Chichester: Wiley and Sons.
Laschinger, Heather and Boss, Marvin (1984) 'Learning styles of nursing students and career choices'. *Journal of Advanced Nursing*. 9, pages 375–80.
Laschinger, Heather (1986). 'Learning styles of nursing students and environmental press perceptions of two clinical nursing settings'. *Journal of Advanced Nursing*. 11, pages 289–94.
Ostmoe, Patricia, Van-Hoozer, Helen, Scheffel, Annette, and Cromwell, Carolyn (1984). 'Learning style preferences and selection of learning strategies: consideration and implications for nurse education'. *Journal of Nursing Education*. Vol. 23, 1, pages 27–30.
Page, Terry, Thomas, J. B., with Marshall, A. R. (1977). *International Dictionary of Education*. London: Kogan Page Ltd.
Pask, G., and Scott, B. E. (1972). 'Learning strategies and individual competence'. *International Journal of Man Machine Studies*. 4, pages 217–53.
Piaget, Jean (1984). 'Intellectual development' in Hayes, Nicky, *A First Choice in Psychology*. Walton-on-Thames: Nelson.
Robinson, Francis (1970). *Effective Study*. London: Harper and Row.

CHAPTER EIGHT

FACILITATION STRATEGIES – THE KEY TO DEVELOPING CLINICAL EXCELLENCE

INTRODUCTION

The act of facilitating is implicit in the nursing role. By facilitating the nurse promotes health, relieves pain, enables a patient to return home, and a learner to move on to the next stage in her training. Facilitation is therefore concerned with making things possible for another, through a process which makes it simpler for that person to achieve her goal. The skills involved in this process are primarily dependent on the task in hand, but also on the needs of the patient or learner and the skills of the facilitator.

FACILITATOR 'QUALITIES'

The facilitator
From the beginning of a child's life its relationships, with mother initially then other family members, play an important part in the way it learns about the world and ways of responding to it. The establishment of a warm loving relationship with the mother or mother substitute has been shown to be important for the normal development of a child and its subsequent intellectual ability (Winnicott, Rutter). However Margaret Donaldson in *Children's Minds* who acknowledges that babies may learn because certain acts lead to rewards, also describes evidence which states that even at this early stage 'babies will learn to behave in ways that produce results in a world with no reward except the successful outcome'. She suggests that humans and animals have an innate desire to learn.

As adults, facilitating adult learners, we recognize that the desire to learn rests in both facilitator and learner but also that what each brings to the relationship varies with the individuals themselves, their educational and life experiences, as well as the present situation. As with the mother-child relationship, a good facilitator-learner alliance stems from a facilitator who accepts his role as a teacher and has the ability to facilitate learning.

The facilitator is aware that each person is a unique being with his or her own biological, psychological social and spiritual needs; that each person has basic needs common to all individuals and has the right to dignity, worth and autonomy. He is aware that each person is constantly interacting with a changing environment in which he strives to maintain homeostasis and in which he responds to internal and external stimuli as a total individual. The facilitator is also aware of the importance of maintaining an active and continuous approach to teaching and learning himself and that he acts as a role model for the learner. At a personal level the facilitator may find it helpful to reflect on his general feelings, thoughts and behaviour towards the learner.

The learner

As has been discussed elsewhere (Chapters Three and Four) the learner is ultimately responsible for her own learning. She is required to participate in the learning process and be motivated and self appraising. She is required to use a number of different methods to meet learning objectives and to be aware that learning occurs in a wide variety of settings.

Traditionally however nurses believe they are 'taught in a classroom' and 'learn on the ward'. To add to this confusing situation the roles of both nurse teachers and registered nurses in the clinical field in recent years have become less differentiated and increasingly they are seeking to encourage learners to take more responsibility for their own learning through the process of facilitation. The nurse teacher has become less prescriptive, and is less concerned with the giving of information in the sense that one might tell a child. He aims to promote problem-solving skills and a preparedness for the reality of clinical caring. The registered nurse working in a clinical setting is aware of finite material resources which, coupled with a faster throughput of patients in acute settings and learners requiring supervision and assessment, is changing the perception and execution of the role. It is therefore even more imperative that all nurses develop the skills of facilitation and in so doing encourage learners to take more responsibility for their own learning and for gaining the most out of different experiences.

The qualities a facilitator requires range from a knowledge of self and skills in inter-personal relationships, to an understanding of the structure within which both facilitator and learner function and the rights, responsibilities, privileges and expectations this may involve. Through these qualities and the knowledge, skill and attitude that they encompass, the facilitator is enabled to assist the learner to identify her needs and to develop strategies which will fulfil these.

IDENTIFICATION OF LEARNER NEEDS

The process of identifying a learner's needs arises out of an initial meeting in which the learner and the facilitator spend time together. The experience of the meeting will be most beneficial to both facilitator and learner if the facilitator takes some responsibility for the following:

1. Making time available.
2. Finding a place to meet.
3. Being aware of the requirements of e.g. the course, assignments etc.

He may usefully encourage the learner to do the following:

1. Bring assignment details, objectives.
2. Think about the task.
3. Identify obvious difficulties.

Although the needs of learners vary enormously depending on the task, the process of facilitation may be surprisingly similar.

Written assignments

Phase 1 - Preparation
The facilitator should endeavour to be familiar with the learner's task – being available and by ensuring that they are unlikely to be disturbed shows his concern for the learner but more importantly *respect* – both for the person and the process. The facilitator should endeavour to be familiar with the learner's task – being especially aware of cut off dates, word-limits, penalties, referencing systems, ethical and resource implications. He will find it useful to obtain a copy of and be familiar with the criteria by which marks are awarded as well as the philosophy of the course.

Phase 2 - The first meeting
At this stage the main objective for the facilitator is to ascertain what the learner thinks and feels about the assignment, being aware that she may already have her own thoughts and feelings. Because the meeting involves the facilitator, it can of course be influenced by his behaviour, for example the facilitator may think that: the assignment seems interesting, is a subject he feels needs to be considered more by nurses, it may represent a challenge to the system, he knows that a lot has been written about the topic. The behaviour he demonstrates will be one of eagerness, enthusiasm, commitment and challenge. The learner however may come to the meeting with other expectations as well as anxieties which the facilitator should be alert to.

Learner expectations
The learner's expectations will seem reasonable to her. She will expect her facilitator to be conversant with the task she has to complete and that he will assist her in the process. She will expect her facilitator to be knowledgeable about the subject, professional in his approach and aware of the difficulties she may experience in identifying and obtaining the relevant information and how to overcome this. She will expect his genuine support and commitment and his acknowledgement of her reasons for pursuing the task. Another aspect of the learner's behaviour may be less explicit and something of which she is unaware,

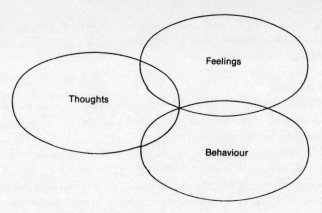

Fig. 8.1 A simple model of self, based on Burnard (1985)

since it is an unconscious process. However it may be linked with her expectations and concerns the phenomenon of projection.

A projection is a device that we use in interpreting our environment, it gives meaning to events. For example, seeing the sun setting over the sea will be interpreted by people in a wide variety of ways depending on the people themselves, who they are with, where, when and why.

Projection is also a term used by most people in an attempt to deal with their own shortcomings – by seeing these in others and denying them in themselves. By projection is meant the tendency to attribute to other people, emotions, ideas or attitudes which they do not in fact possess, but which originate in themselves. Almost any characteristic can be projected onto another. People in love usually initially project an ideal of the opposite sex onto the other person. The learner may project the ideal of 'facilitator' or 'teacher' onto the other, or she may project something equally unreal in a negative sense. The facilitator learns to recognize these projections by being aware of their being inappropriate, of not belonging to him.

The concept of the self and the notion of self-awareness have from time immemorial interested philosophers, theologians and more recently psychologists, social workers and nurses. Burnard describes a simple model of self as comprising thoughts, feelings and behaviour (Fig. 8.1).

Thoughts are processes which contribute to our mental life – processes by which we solve problems, remember and perceive. Feelings are aspects of ourselves expressed for example as apathy, love, empathy, pride and failure. It is from thoughts and feelings that behaviour emerges. It is also through changes in one of these three aspects that the person as a whole may change through processes as varied as behaviour modification, psychoanalysis and humanistic psychology.

What the facilitator remembers of his own learning experiences, how he perceives the motivation of learners today, will influence both what he feels about teaching and learning (himself and in relation to the learner) as well as how he personally behaves in a teaching environment, and the type of environment he will create for the learner.

Learner anxieties

Anxiety also may stem from the self, relationships with others or the environment in which the task is set. The learner may feel a failure; she may feel competent. She may think that the assignment is a useful and valuable subject to consider, or be unable to recognize an aspect of the topic which is meaningful for her. The learner may arrive early or late for the meeting; she may wish to leave before or after the agreed time. Where she chooses to sit, what she actually brings with her, helps the facilitator to ascertain what the learner thinks and feels she needs from him.

During this meeting the facilitator begins to explore with the learner her thoughts and feelings about her assignment – specifically those aspects which he suggested the learner consider prior to their meeting. However it may also be valuable or seem appropriate to allow the learner to talk about other issues since if these are important to the learner they may also influence her approach to the learning process.

Developing rapport with the learner involves confidentiality, empathy, openness, genuineness and warmth – skills more usually associated with counselling but which the facilitator will recognize as enabling for the learner and himself. Allowing the learner to express her expectations and anxieties occurs in an atmosphere of *trust*. The attempts of the facilitator to hear what is being said and to respect and respond to this will enhance the process of trust-building and may also help the learner to start forming a working relationship with the facilitator.

Phase 3 – Clarification of learner needs

The initial meeting opens with facilitator and learner each having certain expectations and anxieties about the task to which they have agreed to commit themselves. Through *active listening* the facilitator will identify the learner's needs. These may usefully be grouped into aspects concerned with thought, feeling and behaviour.

Thought processes

Among the issues about which the learner expresses concern may be the ability to obtain, organize, make sense of and synthesize knowledge. She may express difficulties or a lack of skill in approaches to learning, remembering, attending to and perceiving. The role of the facilitator is to clarify which needs the learner thinks she has, so that the appropriate strategy to meet these is identified. For example if the learner is unsure of how to approach a particular subject it may be because she is unaware of how other people have approached it. Showing her how to do this, by suggesting she looks up the subject in the nursing bibliographies may enable her to obtain the necessary information on which she can make a decision herself.

Difficulty in organizing work may be alleviated by using the learner's previous assignments and offering suggestions as to ways of strengthening the structure and clarifying an argument. Identifying the learner's current skills in learning, remembering, attending to and perceiving, encourages the facilitator to reflect on his own performance as a source of new suggestions for the learner.

Feelings

Like thoughts, a learner's feelings will influence her ability to write an assignment. The facilitator may find it helpful to repeat a feeling that the learner has expressed. For example in the course of the initial meeting the learner may describe herself as being 'tired', 'exhausted', 'excited', 'daunted', 'anxious', 'unsure'. The facilitator may reflect back to the learner 'you feel tired'. This encourages the learner to be specific about her tiredness and enables the facilitator to consider strategies with the learner which may alleviate the feeling of being tired. She may feel tired at the sight of the assignments, because she can't get off to sleep at nights, because she is working in a physically demanding clinical area, because she has been asked to talk about the topic to some students in the School of Nursing. The facilitator can usefully discuss with the learner specific reasons for her feeling of tiredness and, if it seems appropriate, how she experiences her feeling of tiredness and offer some suggestions as to the strategies she might consider as alternatives.

Behaviour

The learner may express anxiety in relation to her ability to 'do' a 'contract', to read all the literature, to write legibly, to present her assignment to the group, to talk about, for example sexuality.

How a person behaves is intimately related to how she thinks and feels. The ability to 'do a contract' may be associated with the learner's perception of the task, her skills in assimilating a new style of learning, her feelings about doing something unfamiliar; or it may arise from a difficulty she experiences in focusing on and considering a topic in some detail. The facilitator can help the learner by encouraging her to be specific about her needs and through an understanding of the learner's difficulties may offer alternative frameworks. In this instance the facilitator would acknowledge the fact that the learner feels uncertain but also offer some concrete information to assist the learner in beginning to understand what is being expected of her and identifying this in an action plan.

Phase 4 – The action plan

At the close of the initial meeting the learner and facilitator will be able to identify a number of needs. These will primarily be learner needs but the facilitator may be aware that he also has specific needs in relation to the assignment. It is most useful to write down the learner's needs, to specify the action agreed and to set a review date. For example a student nurse's task is to do a learning contract of not less that 1000 words on the theme, 'The management of ward resources'.

The learner's needs may be identified and defined as outlined in Table 8.1. Identifying a review date is not only a way of the facilitator and learner committing themselves to doing the agreed task but also of structuring the process. In the action plan in Table 8.1 the facilitator helped the learner to complete the assignment successfully by encouraging her to organize her learning in an efficient, logical and helpful way. This process will encourage the learner not only to understand how to use learning resources – including the facilitator – but also will assist her to assume increasing responsibility for planning her learning and organizing what needs to be learned in relation to the task and her difficulties with it. It encourages the learner to make decisions about learning strategies and resources, which will extend her knowledge and facilitate taking the perspective of others who have alternative ways of understanding into account.

The final phase in the facilitating process is evaluation. This will be reviewed after a short excursion into the area of practical assessments.

Table 8.1 Action plan

Need/problem	Action	Review date
1. Difficulty in formulating objectives for contract	(a) Learner practises using framework of skills, knowledge and attitudes learned in class	
	(b) Learner reads contract objectives written by ward SN doing Diploma in Professional Nursing Studies (DPNS)	
	(c) Discuss (a) and (b) with facilitator	
2. Feeling unsure of ability to do contract	(a) Facilitator agrees specific times to talk with student	
	(b) Learner agrees to write objectives for two contracts on subjects of choice	
	(c) Learner plans times for study	
	(d) Learner negotiates to spend time with manager of choice	
3. Limited knowledge of subject	(a) Learner visits library and identifies four topics and discusses with facilitator	
	(b) Learner identifies four resources on ward	
	(c) Facilitator works with learner and clarifies aspects of contract title in clincal area	

Practical assessments

Phase 1 – Preparation
Preparing for a first meeting with a learner prior to doing a practical assessment is similar to that described for written assignments. Respect for the learner and the process she is undergoing are fundamental to a positive learner-facilitator relationship. The facilitator should be familiar with the practical assessment in general, but especially be aware of the availability of the experience and the supervisory expertise in the clinical area. Among the factors to be considered here therefore are holidays and periods of night duty which the facilitator may have planned, as well as the learner's designated study days and night duty experience.

Phase 2 – The first meeting
As with the written assignments, at this stage the facilitator's main objective is to ascertain what the learner thinks and feels about the assessment and to gauge her experience of previous practical assessments. For example the learner may feel she has 'never been assessed' or 'has been over-assessed'. This may be a reflection of her relationships with any more senior nurse, including the facilitator, or it may refer to her lack of experience in a formal setting. Again the facilitator will be aware of his own experiences (or lack of them) of this assessment, if not as a learner himself then as a result of facilitating other learners. He should nevertheless encourage the learner to express her expectations and anxieties and be alert to any projections.

Learner expectations. The learner's expectations of her facilitator are that she will be enabled to pass the assessment. Essentially this involves his expressed commitment to be a role model for her, and by indicating his understanding of the task and clearly demonstrating a correlation between items on the assessment form and his own knowledge, skills and attitudes. The facilitator may become aware of the level of the learner's expectations, whether for example she 'just wants to pass' or whether she is approaching this as part of the wider preparation for her chosen goal.

Learner anxieties. A learner's anxiety about a practical assessment also reflects her feelings about herself, her relationships with others including patients, but especially those in authority and the setting in which the assessment takes place. Her anxiety will also stem perhaps to an even greater extent than in written assignments, from her previous experience. For example, a learner preparing for her first practical assessment will have a number of life and work experiences of being judged. She will be aware of what has been written about her on ward reports or profiles, what has been said to her in connection with these and how she feels about these. She will also be aware of how her own peers are faring and where she is in relation to them. She will nevertheless have no 'here and now' experience of being formally judged on her practical and inter-personal skills by a registered nurse. The fear of not knowing is universal and can be usefully acknowledged by the facilitator, as can his role during the actual assessment. In considering the setting in which the assessment will occur it is important to be aware of the implications for the nurse and the profession which ensue from success or failure. A learner preparing for her third attempt at her first practical assessment may be most concerned with the implications of failure. The role of the facilitator needs therefore to be firmly focused on the task as well as the learner's fears about the future, doubts about self and ability to trust others.

Phase 3 - Clarification of learner needs
Thought processes. The issues about which the learner may express concern will centre on remembering, learning, attending to and perceiving. For example the learner may find it difficult to remember a procedure, or to learn the effects of a number of drugs. She may lack confidence in attending to more than one person or task at a time; she may lack skill in recognizing changes in a clinical observation.

Feelings. Feelings of anxiety about passing the assessment are quite natural. They stem from the ultimate goal of wanting to complete training successfully, of keeping up with peers and of personal pride. However anxiety which manifests itself in for example anorexia, tremor and insomnia is inappropriate and may suggest the learner is generally lacking in confidence or not yet ready to prepare for the assessment. By acknowledging the learner's anxiety the facilitator may help reduce it. The 'cocky' student may also be expressing anxiety but in a way that is generally seen as less acceptable - by recognizing the feeling behind the behaviour the facilitator is more able to help the learner develop strategies to alleviate her sense of anxiety.

Behaviour. A learner under stress in a practical situation may be aware that she behaves differently. It is common to talk, walk and generally do things quicker, this allows less time for thought, reflection and the normal air of concern. Her feelings of anxiety to 'pass', 'get everything done', 'remember', may result in clumsy, noisy and abrupt action. In trying to remember, she will forget, in watching for, she may not see. The facilitator can help the learner by suggesting she slows down, by encouraging her to be specific about the skills which she finds less easy to do smoothly.

Phase 4 - The action plan
Table 8.2 is an action plan for a third year student nurse doing an Enrolled Nurse (General) to Registered General Nurse, Conversion Course. She is preparing for an assessment which involves her making 'an assessment of and care plan for a surgical patient, which will be implemented during a full tour of duty and providing a written evaluation of the care given'.

Table 8.2 Action plan for a surgical ward

Need/problem	Action	Review date
1. Difficulty in writing problems concisely for long stay patients	(a) Learner practises assisting patients to describe their problems	
	(b) Learner role plays being a patient with peer in class	
	(c) Learner role plays being nurse with peer patient, in class	
	(d) Facilitator discusses learner care plan with learner on ward and reviews other care plan with learner	
2. To use assessment form appropriately for short stay patients	(a) Facilitator obtains short stay form from wards using them	
	(b) Facilitator discusses with learner and identifies important features	
	(c) Learner uses short stay format on ward with sister's permission	
	(d) Facilitator discusses assessment with learner, on ward	
3. Difficulty in describing evaluation of care given	(a) Learner revises principles of evaluating care (own textbook and notes from class)	
	(b) Facilitator works with learner and assists in phrasing of evaluation	
	(c) Learner discusses written evaluation with peers in class	

This particular learner had no difficulty talking with patients, so by encouraging her to seek their help actively in formulating their problems, she learned how to express these on paper. By working with the learner (3b) the facilitator would be encouraging her to implement the written care plan and to identify the expected outcomes. For example:

Problem	Activity	Evaluation
Unable to maintain normal hygiene needs	Assist patient with hygiene needs	Patient assisted to wash basin. Able to wash face hands and front trunk. Nurse did remainder. Patient felt tired but refreshed and pleased with progress.

Again the facilitator encouraged the learner to organize her learning by suggesting review dates that would contribute to a logical and efficient use of time.

FACILITATOR STRATEGIES

So far in this chapter it has been suggested that the facilitator needs to demonstrate *respect* for the learner and the process she is involved in, to establish a climate of *trust* with the learner, and to identify through *active listening* the learner's needs in relation to written and practical work. A number of examples of problems which the learner may experience have been identified and so it is the intention now to consider in more detail strategies which the facilitator may choose in order that he identify these more readily.

John Heron in *Dimensions of Facilitator Style* identifies six dimensions that group facilitators may use depending on the perceived needs of a group at a particular time. These are derived from his six category intervention analysis. Each dimension comprises a pair of styles neither of which is more or less valuable than the other. They reflect degrees of facilitator or group intervention. The interventions are described as:

1. Directive .... Nondirective.
   (prescriptive)
2. Interpretative .... Noninterpretative.
   (informative)
3. Confronting .... Nonconfronting.
4. Carthartic .... Noncarthartic.
5. Structuring .... Nonstructuring.
   (catalytic)
6. Disclosing .... Nondisclosing.
   (supportive)

Some of these styles reflect *what* the facilitator does to the group process, (for example structuring), while others (for example directive), reflect *how* he does it.

The facilitator may use any one of these styles in assisting an individual learner with her particular task.

1. The directive-nondirective intervention

These styles refer to the poles of the dimension. They refer to a situation in which the facilitator either prescribes what the learner will do (directive) or facilitates the learner to decide for herself (nondirective). For instance, the facilitator is being directive in telling the learner to look up specific information relating to her assignment or if he suggests how she might begin to approach the task.

He is being nondirective during the meeting by actively encouraging the learner to use her initiative and to accept or reject his proposals according to their relevance and appropriateness to her needs and interests.

2. The interpretative-noninterpretative dimension
These styles directly reflect the facilitator's skill in understanding what is happening in relation to the learner and her task. He may offer a suggestion which can help increase understanding of this (interpretative/informative) or he may ask the learner to do this, (noninterpretative). For example the learner may feel that her previous experience of being watched in a practical setting has been limited because: 'Sister never seemed to put me on with my facilitator'. The facilitator himself may suggest that the learner is attributing Sister's behaviour as a deliberate intent to be unhelpful thereby compounding the learner's lack of experience, or that Sister had other equally unhelpful motives for this. He may ask the learner to suggest why this situation occurred: 'What do you feel Sister intended by this', 'Why would she do such a thing?'. By structuring the discussion the facilitator encourages the learner to express her thoughts and feelings. This process will raise her awareness of other factors which affect decisions about, for example, off duty, as well as the learner's need to assert her needs and take responsibility for her learning experiences. The facilitator is being interpretative by attributing psychological meaning to intent, motives and types of statement. He is being noninterpretative by encouraging the learner to reflect on her own and others' verbal and nonverbal behaviour and to bring meaning to the situation.

3. The confronting-nonconfronting dimension
This dimension is concerned with the facilitator challenging the learner's behaviour, beliefs or attitudes when these appear to be disenabling. This can be brought about by the facilitator being very critical of the learner's behaviour. For example a learner may on more than one occasion fail to produce work which she is finding difficult to complete for the facilitator to discuss with her. Her behaviour indicates her anxiety, and a suggestion that the facilitator could be more helpful. The facilitator may direct her to bring the work to him and express his feelings of frustration at her suggestion that he is not being helpful, since he feels this is not only distoring but manipulating the situation. By stating his experience and impressions of the learner's behaviour the facilitator is giving her direct feedback but does so in a way that is supportive – by asking her to bring the work so that he can be helpful and not undermining her actual efforts.

The facilitator's skill in remembering what the learner has said, for example in talking about her attitudes to patients, can be used to confront the learner about inconsistencies in her attitudes. These may be defensive or rigid and restrict the possibility of learning. By questioning about the incompatibility between two statements the learner will become more aware of her own beliefs. Being overtly confronting can be a useful strategy to employ when there are inconsistencies in behaviour, attitudes and beliefs.

The use of silence by the facilitator is an example of nonconfrontation. Being silent shifts the responsibility for working out what to do onto the learner. This may be experienced as confronting and threatening by the learner but the facilitator's non-threatening, non-verbal cues will help the learner to begin to use the space positively.

4. The cathartic-noncathartic dimension

This dimension is concerned with the release of feeling through for example, sobbing, shaking and laughing. It usually arises after one or more other interventions have been used and is one through which considerable insight may be gained. The inexperienced facilitator may find he has precipitated this experience as he becomes aware of being or having been overly critical of learner's behaviour. He may realize for example that *he* has distorted some of the facts and has been inappropriately angered by the learner. The learner's behaviour from being mildly aggressive or defensive, may become exaggerated, wildly alarmed, incensed with anger, overtly hostile and unable to hold back a tumult of frustration and tears. Although the facilitator may rightly feel that he has 'caused this' he also recognizes that the learner's behaviour is an acting out of feeling which in similar situations she has been unable to express but which at this time he is allowing her to do.

For catharsis to occur the facilitator gives his permission – either before or as it is happening – 'It's alright to cry'. He picks up verbal and non-verbal cues. The learner who says 'I don't know why I am doing this' may not just be referring to the assignment. Changing her position, putting her head down and hands over her eyes, or walking around the room and looking out of the window may be non-verbal cues that indicate a change of mind too. The learner's distress on having suddenly acquired a painful insight may be quite shattering. The facilitator will probably assist the learner most at this time by being still and not moving to comfort her. This strength in being still will be communicated to the learner and help her in accepting the reality of the situation. By moving towards the learner the facilitator is changing his position; he may be interfering, 'I'm sorry I didn't mean to hurt you'. In which case this could diffuse the cathartic experience and prevent the learner from gaining insight from it.

Encouraging her to talk about how the insight will affect the situation will probably be of more help to her. When catharsis has occurred the facilitator can be actively noncathartic and encourage the learner to come back into the present by helping her to focus on some positive achievements and strengths.

Catharsis is a powerful experience for facilitator and learner and if handled with skill and sensitivity can be a point of personal growth for both.

5. The structuring-unstructuring dimension

This dimension involves the extent to which the facilitator acts as a catalyst. Catalytic intervention refers to the way the facilitator structures the interaction in order that the learner is encouraged to be self-directed and to discover things for and about herself. This style is therefore explicitly concerned with how the facilitator develops these skills in the learner. He may do this by being structuring or unstructuring. Being structuring can occur in one or more ways. The facilitator may choose to clarify with the learner the philosophy of the school or course and responsibilities of each to them. These ground rules may be supplemented by him confirming his role. Depending on the level of the learner, the facilitator will do this by acting as a role model, by ensuring that the learner seeks theoretical explanations for her practice, by providing support when the learner is required to practise clinical skills, by assisting the learner to think in concepts rather than tasks, by actively participating in her assignment and by providing a written report on her progress. In defining his role the facilitator is also identifying his limits and sharing his feelings about the nature of the facilitating process.

In effect he is offering a contract which the learner accepts or rejects. By entering into the contract the learner is encouraged to define her expectations and anxieties, but more importantly to make the choice about whether this learning experience is consistent with her expectations and to take responsibility for this. Another aspect of structuring concerns the environment in which the initial meeting occurs – where, for how long and at what time, will each affect the learner's perception of facilitation and will reflect the facilitator's commitment. In being unstructuring, the facilitator provides resources from which the learner chooses according to her perceived needs, for example, a reading list, audio visual aids, specialist personnel, role play. The extent to which the facilitator suggests *what* might be most useful defines the degree of structure. Self directed learning is therefore most clearly reflected in an unstructured style.

Contract Structuring. The contract-structuring described above is an example of the overlap between two dimensions – directions and structuring. In contract structuring the facilitator is both proposing *how* learning will occur (directive) and *what* he can contribute to the process (structuring).

6. *The disclosing-nondisclosing dimension*

The styles in this dimension are concerned with the facilitator in a supportive role and the extent to which he is self-disclosing. Self-disclosure occurs when the facilitator expresses his personal beliefs about for example, what the learner is currently studying. He offers them in a genuine desire to help the learner, as a result of his own study and experience.

He may share real experiences which have influenced his life in an attempt to assist the learner in understanding or gaining insight. At an appropriate time these may usefully include not only difficult and distressing events, but also the rare moments of insight and ingenuity – and the pain and joy which these involve. In being disclosing, the facilitator is being authentic, he is concerned with self rather than role. Through being disclosing the facilitator affirms his own worth but also encourages the learner to do the same. He shows respect for her rights, honours her needs and enhances her confidence.

Being nondisclosing gives the responsibility for self-disclosure to the learner. The facilitator expresses his support by giving his time and attention but remains silent. He communicates his care by non-verbal means – posture, facial expression – which, together with not feeling anxious himself, will communicate to the learner a sense of space which she can fill with whatever she chooses to disclose – at whatever level.

Having briefly explored the six dimensions the facilitator needs to make some decisions not only about when to use each, but also how effective he is in relation to assisting the learner.

EVALUATION OF FACILITATOR STYLE

Evaluation strategies in relation to the theory and practice of adult education have been discussed in detail in Chapter Six. Evaluation of facilitator style is specifically concerned with what was achieved – *outcome,* and how it was achieved – *process,* in relation to the learner and facilitator himself.

Table 8.3 Evaluation of outcome

---

1. **Written assignments**
   (a) Adequacy of information about the task including:
       i Title
       ii Criteria for assessment/grading scheme
       iii Word limit/penalties
       iv Cut off date
       v Preferred referencing system
       vi Availability of resources
   (b) Relevance of chosen subject to the learner including:
       i Present clinical relevance
       ii Breadth and depth of knowledge
       iii Availability of appropriate literary resources
       iv Accessibility of human resources
       v Potential for future use/development
       vi Relationship to other aspects of the course

2. **Practical assessments**
   (a) Adequacy of information about the task including:
       i Criteria for assessment
       ii Cut off date
       iii Availability of suitable experience
   (b) Relevance of chosen skill to the learner including:
       i Present clinical experience
       ii Ability to practise with supervision
       iii Ability to apply skill to other tasks

Outcome

The explicit most desired outcome for the learner is the sucessful completion of the task. There are however a number of factors which the facilitator may choose to explore with the learner in order to increase his and the learner's understanding of what has been achieved in this particular educational experience (Table 8.3).

The facilitator will be aware that various factors can influence the learner's response to even a formal evaluation, notably when it is given in relation to the outcome, where, and the reasons for giving it. An informal evaluation will also be influenced by the facilitator's relationship to the learner and the extent to which the latter finds her needs and expectations have been met. It is important however that he acknowledges the learner's responses are particular to her, and that as her

Table 8.4 Evaluation of the Process

1. **Written assignments**
   (a) Adequacy of preparation for the task including initial meeting – time, place, requirements
   (b) Adequacy of the action plan including:
       (i) Identified problems and actions
       (ii) Review dates
       (iii) Specific strategies in relation to learner's difficulties with thought processes, feelings, behaviour
       (iv) Identification of future needs
   (c) Use and appropriateness of facilitator strategies:
       (i) Directive – nondirective (prescriptive)
       (ii) Interpretative – noninterpretative (informative)
       (iii) Confronting – nonconfronting
       (iv) Cathartic – noncathartic
       (v) Structuring – nonstructuring (catalytic)
       (vi) Disclosing – nondisclosing (supportive)

2. **Practical assessments**
   (a) Adequacy in preparation for the task including initial meeting – time, place, requirements
   (b) Adequacy of the action plan including:
       (i) Identification of problems and actions
       (ii) Review dates
       (iii) Availability of experience
       (iv) Supervised experience
       (v) Identification of future needs
   (c) Use and appropriateness of facilitator strategies
       (i) Directive – nondirective (prescriptive)
       (ii) Interpretative – noninterpretative (informative)
       (iii) Confronting – nonconfronting
       (iv) Cathartic – noncathartic
       (v) Structuring – nonstructuring (catalytic)
       (vi) Disclosing – nondisclosing (supportive)

facilitator a proportion of her responses will vary according to her specific needs, and therefore that any major revision in his role is considered in this light. The facilitator will find it valuable to consider as part of his performance review, his own strengths and weaknessess in assisting the learner to achieve her outcome.

Process
Evaluating the process which has occurred is essential for the facilitator, but will be most useful to him if this is considered with the learner. This involves evaluation of the phases and strategies. A format for this is suggested in Table 8.4.

CONCLUSION
The chapter began by suggesting that facilitation is 'concerned with making things possible for another through a process which makes it simpler for that person to achieve his goal'. By identifying that this process encompasses not only what the facilitator does but how he may fulfil this role, it is clear that facilitating strategies may be diverse and demanding. However the experience of being a facilitator is also potentially satisfying and valuable to the individual's personal development. Among the significant experiences which the facilitator may perceive as being valuable are the following:

1. Commanding credibility which does not depend solely on status; earning respect through the exercise of personal ability and attitudes.
2. Ability to extract the maximum contribution from individual students; helping students work within defined objectives to strict time limits.
3. Acting as a role model; exhibiting behaviour and attitudes which accommodate new ideas about the practice of nursing.
4. Experience of concentrated individual counselling.

TOPICS FOR DISCUSSION
1. Reflect on your personal strengths and weaknesses in relation to facilitating learners, then discuss these with peers.
2. Identify at least two examples of difficulties that learners have expressed in relation to thoughts, feelings and behaviour concerning written and practical work.
3. How might you build trust with and gain a learner's respect?
4. Consider a second year student preparing for her 'total patient care practical assessment'. What factors would you discuss with her?
5. A sister/charge nurse selects you to be their facilitator during the DPNS Course. What decisions will you need to make before agreeing to this?

REFERENCES

Abercrombie, M. J. L. (1960). *The Anatomy of Judgement*. Harmondsworth: Penguin.

Beckett, C. and Wall, M. (1985). 'Role of the clinical facilitator', *Nurse Education Today* 3, pages 259–62.

Bond, M. (1986). *Stress and Self-Awareness: A Guide for Nurses*. London: William Heinemann Medical Books.

Bridge, G. E. and MacLeod Clark, J. (1981). *Communication in Nursing Care*. H. M. & M. Publishers Ltd.

Burnard, P. (1985). *Learning Human Skills: A Guide for Nurses*. London: Heinemann Nursing.

Cassee, E. (1975). 'Therapeutic behaviour, hospital culture and communication' in Cox, C., and Mead, A. (eds) *A Sociology of Medical Practice*. London: Collier-MacMillan.

Davis, E. D. (ed.) (1983). *Research into Nurse Education*. Beckenham: Croom Helm Ltd.

Donaldson, M. (1978). *Children's Minds*. London: Fontana.

Egan, G. (1985). *Exercises in Helping Skills*. Monterey California: Brooks/Cole Publishing Company.

Egan, G. (1986). *The Skilled Helper*. Monterey California: Brooks/Cole Publishing Company.

Hand, L. (1981). *Nursing Supervision*. Virginia USA: Reston Publishing Company Inc.

Hargie, O., Saunders, C. and Dickson, D. (1981). *Social Skills In Interpersonal Communication*. Beckenham: Croom Helm Ltd.

Heron, J. (1977). *Dimensions of Facilitator Style*. British Post-Graduate Medical Federation (University of London) in association with Human Potential Research Project – Departement of Adult Education, University of Surrey.

Jarvis, P., and Gibson, S. (1985). *The Teacher Practitioner in Nursing, Midwifery and Health Visiting*. London: Croom Helm.

Knowles, M. (1973). *The Adult Learner: A Neglected Species*. Houston: Golf Publishing.

Meizirow, J. (1983). 'A critical theory of adult learning and education', cited in Tight, M. (ed.) *Adult Learning and Education*. London: Croom Helm/Open University.

Pollock, M. (1983). *Patient Assessment of Nursing Care*. (MPhil Thesis). University of Southampton.

Porritt, L. (1984). *Communication: Choices For Nurses*. Edinburgh: Churchill Livingstone.

Rogers, C. R. (1969). *Freedom to Learn*. Columbus Ohio: Mernie.

Rutter, M. (1972). *Maternal Deprivation Re-Assessed*. Harmondsworth: Penguin.

Storr, A. (1968). *Human Aggression*. London: Pelican Books.

Tschudin, V. (1982). *Counselling Skills For Nurses*. Eastbourne: Bailliere Tindall.

Winnicott, D. W. (1964). *The Child, The Family and The Outside World*. Harmondsworth: Penguin.

CHAPTER NINE

ASSESSMENT AND PROFILING OF CLINICAL PERFORMANCE

INTRODUCTION

Clinical performance is difficult to judge fairly. Historically, clinical assessment has looked for what is 'wrong' with the students' performance. This chapter describes a new approach to the difficult matter of assessing clinical practice.

> If we wish to discover the truth about an educational system, we must look into its assessment procedures.
>
> (Rowntree, 1977)

Do we agree with Rowntree? If so, what truths would we discover about nurse training and education if we looked into its assessment procedures? Rowntree goes on to ask the following questions of an educational system:

1. What student qualities and achievements are actively valued and rewarded by the system?
2. How are its purposes and intentions realized?
3. To what extent are the hopes and ideals, aims and objectives, professed by the system, ever truly perceived, valued and striven for by *those who make their way within it*? (my italics)

He maintains that the answers to such questions are to be found in what the system of education requires the student to *do* in order to survive and prosper.

ASSESSMENT

In a practice-based profession such as nursing, what the student can *do* at the end of training is of paramount importance. *The Nurses, Midwives, Health Visitors Rules Approval Order* (1983) lists the following competencies that a nurse must achieve before her/his name can be added to the appropriate register:

Training for admission to Parts 1 to 8 of the register

18.- (1) Courses leading to a qualification the successful completion of which shall enable an application to be made for admission to Part 1, 3, 5 or 8 of the register shall provide opportunities to enable the student to accept responsibility for her personal progressional development and to acquire the competencies required to:

(a) advise on the promotion of health and the prevention of illness;
(b) recognize situations that may be detrimental to the health and well-being of the individual;
(c) carry out those activities involved when conducting the comprehensive assessment of a person's nursing requirements;
(d) recognize the significance of the observations made and use these to develop an initial nursing assessment;
(e) devise a plan of nursing care based on the assessment with the co-operation of the patient, to the extent that this is possible, taking into account the medical prescription;
(f) implement the planned programme of nursing care and where appropriate teach and co-ordinate other members of the caring team who may be responsible for implementing specific aspects of the nursing care;
(g) review the effectiveness of the nursing care provided, and where appropriate, initiate any action that may be required;
(h) work in a team with other nurses, and with medical and para-medical staff and social workers;
(i) undertake the management of the care of a group of patients over a period of time and organise the appropriate support services;

related to the care of the particular type of patient with whom she is likely to come into contact when registered in that Part of the register for which the student intends to qualify.

The assessment of student nurses is said to be an estimate of a learner's knowledge, skills and attitudes in relation to pre-determined criteria of *competency*. Fig. 9.1 shows a model adapted from Kehoe and Harker (1979).

The trend now in nurse education is to move away from judging one person against another (norm-referenced assessment), towards specifying what kind of nurse we are trying to develop (criterion-referenced assessment). In recent years a

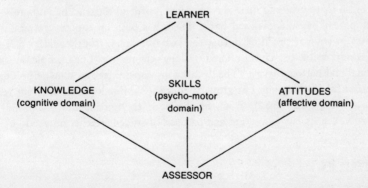

Fig. 9.1 Model of learner/assessor relationship in the light of knowledge, skills and attitudes (after Kehoe and Harker, 1979)

belief has grown that this is best met by continuing assessment rather than one final examination at the end of the course (terminal assessment).

Prior to the the 1970s the terminal assessment of student nurses consisted of two three hour discursive (essay-type) examination papers which tested knowledge; and practical skills assessed far away from the wards, in the School of Nursing practical room, with a bogus patient who was paid ten shillings per examination session. This format was modified by replacing one of the discursive papers by a multiple choice question paper in order to test a wider range of the syllabus, give all students the experience of answering identical questions and introduce more objectivity into marking. A radical step was taken regarding the practical examination by introducing the four-part assessment in a real clinical situation, and using internal assessors drawn from clinical and tutorial staff. This method is still in existence but remains a terminal assessment as each part is dependent upon performance on one particular day.

The next progression in the story of student nurse assessment began in the Spring of 1985 when the English National Board (ENB) began a process to devolve examination procedures for Registered General Nurse courses to Schools of Nursing. Teachers of nursing became internal examiners and had to assume more responsibility for testing the competence of their students and making recommendations concerning pass and fail. External examiners were introduced and given the important remit to monitor and maintain a school's academic and professional standards. This new examination system gives greater autonomy to establishments responsible for the training of nurses. They are made more responsible for the maintenance of standards, and have an opportunity to make positive contributions to curriculum development and the maintenance of the quality of work within a School of Nursing. However, students still work and study for three years towards performing well in one final assessment in order to become registered nurses.

With continuing assessment, information regarding the achievements and attainment by each student is collected and collated regularly throughout a course, so that at the end there is a complete profile of the student's progress and development on an individual basis. There has been an enormous amount of interest in student profiling during the last five years, from a wide variety of bodies responsible for education and training schemes for young people, at local, regional and national levels. 'The "profile movement" shows signs of becoming the most far reaching and fast growing educational development in recent years' (Gloria Hitchcock, 1986). It opens the door to fundamental reappraisal of curricula, assessment procedures and patterns of student-teacher interaction.

PROFILES

A profile is not in itself a method of assessment, it is a document, a means of *recording* assessment across a wide range of student ability, including skills, attitudes, personal qualities and achievements, as well as subject attainments. It can thus be seen that profiling identifies elements to be assessed beyond the narrow cognitive (knowledge) skills which have traditionally formed the basis of assessment in educational courses.

Profiles draw on evidence as alternatives, or additions, to examination results and can therefore reflect a wider range of achievement and experience. They allow for student participation which has a *formative* as well as *summative* function. A formative process is one of recording, reporting and commenting upon a student's work, personal qualities and social skills as she/he progresses. Students can be helped to identify strengths and weaknesses and to develop competence with the principle aim of improving future attainment and development. It is part of the continuing learning process. Summative, on the other hand, refers to an end statement on a student's overall achievement and performance. This may be at the end of an area of study and learning, an allocation, or a three year course. The formative process is thus the 'profiling' referred to in the title of this chapter, whilst the summative product is the 'profile' document itself. A profile, therefore, offers a fuller, more rounded picture of the individual student. Perhaps an analogy can be drawn here with the nursing process giving individualized patient care, and profiles providing equal care and attention regarding individualized student assessment.

There are as many different styles of profile document as there are schools and colleges, and these vary from one sheet of A4 paper to an elaborately bound book. The more complicated ones require separate handbooks as guides to their usage. When developing a profile document for use in student nurse training, careful consideration needs to be given to the large numbers of qualified staff who will be involved in compiling the profiles. These include ward sisters, staff nurses and enrolled nurses, nurse teachers and managers. It is therefore important that the profile is easy to read and understand by all who come into contact with it.

To assess competency during clinical placements a 'graded statement' form of profile, as used by the City and Guilds of London Institute's involvement in the Youth Opportunities Programme, has been successfully adapted and developed by the Dorset School of Nursing (Fig. 9.2). Although a sophisticated format to compile, once in use it is both simple and effective.

Four basic areas of skill and ability are considered.

1. Social abilities.
2. Communication skills.
3. Practical skills.
4. Decision-making abilities.

Each of these areas is sub-divided into two or three categories

1. Social abilities	(a) Working with colleagues.
	(b) Self awareness.
2. Communication skills	(a) Talking and listening.

		1. BASIC LEVEL	2.	3.	4. HIGHEST LEVEL
SOCIAL ABILITIES	WORKING WITH COLLEAGUES	Can co-operate with others when led. Understands and follows simple instructions under supervision.	Can work with other members of a nursing team to achieve common aims and carry out instructions independently.	Understands own position and results of own actions within a ward team.	Is an active, decisive and confident member of a team which incorporates a wide range of hospital personnel.
	SELF AWARENESS	Is aware of own personality and situation.	Can determine own strengths, weaknesses and preferences with guidance.	Has a good basic understanding of own situation, personality and motivation.	Has a thorough understanding of own personality and abilities and their implications.
COMMUNICATION	TALKING AND LISTENING	Can hold conversations face to face and by telephone. Can take accurate messages.	Can follow and give simple descriptions and explanations.	Can communicate effectively with a range of people in a variety of situations.	Shows good insight into verbal and non-verbal communication in differing situations.
	READING AND WRITING	Can identify and understand relevant documents and their purpose.	Can accurately complete selected documents under supervision.	Can effectively complete a variety of documents with minimal supervision.	Can independently select, collate and evaluate relevant written data.
PRACTICAL SKILLS	USING EQUIPMENT	After demonstration, can use basic equipment safely to perform simple procedures.	With guidance can use equipment safely to carry out more complex procedures.	Can select and use suitable equipment and materials for a procedure.	Can set up and maintain equipment and identify/ remedy common faults.
	ASEPTIC TECHNIQUE	After demonstration can prepare a patient and equipment for a simple procedure.	Can safely carry out a specified procedure under supervision.	Is capable of carrying out safe procedures without supervision.	Demonstrates a wide range of knowledge of the theory and practice of asepsis.

DECISION MAKING ABILITIES

ADMINISTRATION OF DRUGS	Can read and interpret prescription sheets correctly.	Under supervision can prepare and administer drugs via the oral route.	Under supervision can carry out a drug round safely and administer drugs via differing routes.	Shows good understanding of the effects and side-effects of a wide range of drugs.
NURSING CARE i. assessment	Can assess basic physical needs under supervision.	Can assess physical and psychological needs under supervision.	Can carry out a complete assessment with minimal supervision.	Can carry out comprehensive assessments and recognise the significance of observation.
ii. planning	Can identify the elements of a care plan.	Can plan care under supervision.	Can plan care and identify priorities with minimal supervision.	Can plan care based upon a comprehensive assessment.
iii. implementing	Can assist in implementing care.	Can implement care under supervision.	Can initiate care with minimal supervision.	Can implement care plans and teach and co-ordinate other members of the team.
iv. evaluating	Can evaluate care given to one patient.	Makes significant contributions to evaluations of care for a group of patients.	Can review the effectiveness of care given.	Can initiate any appropriate changes and action resulting from evaluation.
MANAGEMENT	Has observed and discussed the management of care for a group of patients.	Under supervision can undertake the management of care for a group of patients.	Can undertake the management of care for a group of patients over a period of time.	Can organise the appropriate support services and adapt to a changing situation.
HEALTH EDUCATION	Can identify aspects of healthy living.	Can discuss aspects of health promotion.	Can recognise situations detrimental to the health and wellbeing of the individual.	Can advise on the promotion of health and prevention of illness.

Fig. 9.2 The Dorset School of Nursing student profile for clinical placements

                          (b) Reading and writing.

3. Practical skills   (a) Using equipment.

                          (b) Aseptic technique.

                          (c) Administering drugs.

4. Decision-making abilities   (a) Nursing care.

                          (b) Management.

                          (c) Health education.

Only the nursing care category has been further sub-divided, into the four elements of the nursing process, making a total of thirteen sections on the profile. The student 'grows', or develops, in the profile through four levels in each section, beginning at a basic functioning level through to the highest level expected of a student nurse at the end of three years' training. The competence envisaged at each level is described below.

Level 1 (Basic). Has seen or done x but needs further guidance, experience and supervision.

Level 2. Developing competence at x with help and under supervision.

Level 3. Competent, mostly unaided and needing minimal supervision.

Level 4 (Highest). Competent, unaided and able to help and teach others.

Level 1 has been likened to a 'bud' and Level 4 the fully opened 'flower'! The nine competencies, cited in the Nurses, Midwives and Health Visitors Rules Approval Order (page 161 above), have been incorporated into the highest levels. When a student is deemed completely competent at a given level the appropriate box is shaded and dated (see Fig. 9.3).

iii. imple-menting	Can assist in implementing care. 3.3.87	Can implement care under supervision. 1.4.87	Can initiate care with minimal supervision	Can implement care plans and teach and co-ordinate other members of the team.

Fig. 9.3 An example of one section of the Dorset School of Nursing Profile.

In this type of profile there are no grades or marks, thus making it a positive form of assessment. If a level is not attained, that is, the student is not seen to be completely competent at that level, then she/he remains on the previous one. If the students are not at the basic functioning level then they do not feature on the form and have not begun to 'grow' in that particular section.

Where profiles are part of a continuing assessment for an overall course of education or training, then minimal expected standards must be officially documented and counselling procedures for failure to meet the minimal expected standards clearly defined. A new profile sheet, as seen in Fig. 9.2, is used for each student on every clinical placement, so that she/he begins at the basic levels again for each new allocation. This ensures one of the advantages of continuing assessment, namely, that competency at *all* levels must be demonstrated continuously throughout a course of training, instead of a 'once only' demonstration of skill on 'the day' as seen in terminal assessments.

Student profiling, for the purpose of continuous assessment during clinical placements, immediately replaces two tasks which often prove time-consuming and onerous for qualified ward staff. These are the four-part practical assessment and the 'traditional' nurse's report. Hence, in areas where a single, straightforward profile document has been introduced it has been very welcome. Another advantage of profiles is that they eliminate the need for secrecy and anxiety which can surround the conventional student reporting system. Profile documents are freely accessible to trained staff and students, thus allowing for regular discussion and counselling which can only aid the learning process. Each profile can be likened to an 'individual growth chart'.

As babies attain the 'milestones' of development in their own time and at their own pace, so student nurses can expect to attain competence in the same individual manner. They are not in a race or competition. The onus for recording competence in the profile must fall heavily upon the student and she/he will often initiate progress discussions via the profile.

Profiling is a new concept in nursing training but should make the assessment of ability and skills simpler and more straightforward. In clinical areas the overall responsibility for assessment of students falls heavily upon sisters and charge nurses. However, with a team approach and considerate delegation to staff nurses and enrolled nurses, this load is somewhat lightened, especially where a 'mentor-scheme' is established. A dictionary definition of mentor is 'an experienced and trusted advisor: a wise counsellor'. Each student is allocated to a qualified member of the ward team who becomes her/his mentor. Mentors ensure that their students settle and adapt to the ward and progress and develop professionally during the allocation within a learning environment.

A mentor's role includes the following:

1. Conducting preliminary introduction and orientation to the ward or department.
2. Allowing the student to identify areas where she/he needs help and guidance.
3. Working with the student at least once a week caring for patients allocated to them.
4. Assessing the student's competence and consulting with other trained members of the team regarding performance and progress.
5. Assisting the student to identify and fulfil specific ward objectives.
6. Creating opportunities for discussion and counselling.

Where student profile documents are introduced for assessment in clinical areas these must be seen as just one part of a larger profile of the student which incorporates a wide range of knowledge, skills and attitudes, plus other qualities which were not previously assessed by formal examination. If we assess, and therefore recognize as important, such qualities as initiative, co-operation, communication and inter-personal skills, it is necessary to look at the curriculum and consider whether it affords the opportunity for student nurses to acquire, practise and display such qualities. The formative, interactive nature of profiling calls for a completely different approach to teaching and a relationship with students which will influence the curriculum. Basically, education is assessment-led. If we change the way we look at assessment we need to change our view of the curriculum.

The future of nurse education is moving towards student nurses becoming entirely supernumerary, having true student status and one to two common foundation years. A scheme of training for the general register, incorporating some of these futuristic features, is being piloted by the Dorset School of Nursing. Fig. 9.4 shows a diagrammatic representation of integrated theory and practice during the foundation year of the pilot scheme. This year (Stage 1) consists of

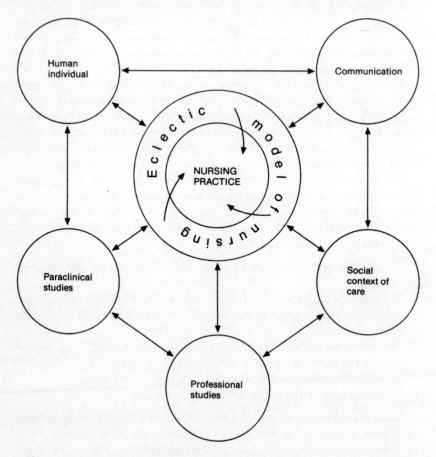

Fig. 9.4 Diagrammatic representation of Stage 1

three academic terms and the students are supernumerary. Continual assessment is by means of context-related essays, two unseen question papers, a research-based project and the attainment of basic levels of competence (except management) in the clinical profile as shown in Fig. 9.2.

During the next two years the students are no longer supernumerary but integrated theory and practice continues, together with assessment. By the end of Stage 2, which is eighteen months (see Fig. 9.5), the students are expected to have gained competence up to level 3 in the profile document, and are academically assessed by an unseen paper and by learning contracts. When undertaking the latter the student chooses to write about specific topics that interest her, under the guidance of a facilitator who is usually a tutor. Student and facilitator agree upon objectives and clearly-defined areas to be covered in the assignment and thus a 'contract' is made between them which the student has to fulfil. During the final

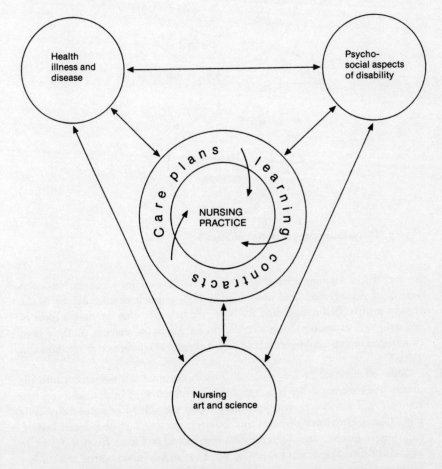

Fig. 9.5 Diagrammatic representation of Stage 2

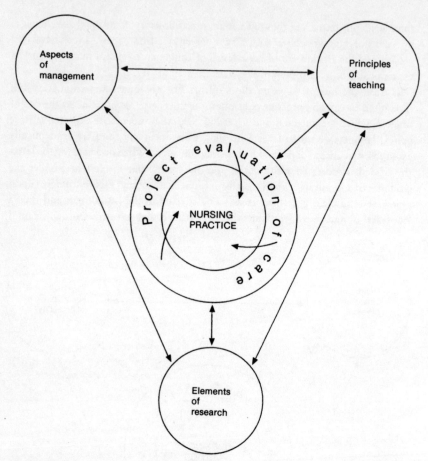

Fig. 9.6 Diagrammatic representation of Stage 3

six months of training (Stage 3) see Fig. 9.6, the students concentrate upon aspects of management and attaining the highest levels of competency in the clinical profile. Before attaining RGN status, however, they produce a piece of research, not exceeding 5,000 words, on an aspect of nursing of their own choosing. The expected outcomes of such a three year course as this are shown in Table 9.1.

Some educational and training schemes incorporate self assessment into the overall assessment profile. It is regarded with suspicion by others, who feel that students' self assessment will inevitably err on the side of being unrealistically high. Gloria Hitchcock disputes this, however, stating that people are, in fact, surprisingly honest, any discrepancies more often occurring from too low an assessment. Self assessment has not, as yet, been widely incorporated into student nurse training; but it has been found useful and beneficial in some areas for

Table 9.1

	Conceptual content	Outcome
Stage 1	Foundations of biological and social sciences	Knowledge base for practice
	Concepts of health and disease	Assessment skills
	Models of nursing	Introduction to care planning
	Interactive skills	Self awareness
	Common nursing techniques	Ability to function as a junior member of the nursing team
Stage 2	Specialist knowledge of pathological processes	Ability to integrate knowledge from biological and social sciences in care planning
	Knowledge of psycho-social aspects of health illness and disability	Able to implement care plans Promotes health
	Application of models of nursing	Competence as a member of the health team
Stage 3	Co-ordination of care	Cares for groups of patients
	Analysis of care plans	Evaluates cares
	Research knowledge	Takes new initiatives and uses originality
	Knowledge to teach	Safe competent and independent practitioner

students to indicate (possibly via a column in a report or profile sheet) what level of achievement they believe they have reached prior to an allocation, and in which areas they feel they need help, supervision and guidance. An example of the self assessment form to be completed at the end of a clinical experience is seen in Table 9.2.

It would be naive to suppose that student-profiling had only advantages over other forms of assessment; it has its share of problems and pitfalls, as most things, but so long as people are aware of these, I believe that profiling is advantageous to assessment procedure.

One problem is subjectivity. The danger of subjective judgments and comments by clinical specialists and nurse teachers must be a major concern for all involved in compiling profiles. When faced with the problem of a 'poor student', the traditional reporting system can prove more damning and distressing, for both student and qualified nurse doing the reporting, than a profile document. Profiling offers ample opportunity to rectify a situation before the 'report' stage as profile documents are more freely available and initiate frequent constructive discussions regarding progress. It is hoped that qualified nurses attempt to be professional and objective at all times.

Table 9.2 Self assessment at the end of an allocation

Think about your work and progress in this area.

1. What have you enjoyed doing most?

2. What do you think you are best at?

3. In which areas have you made the most progress?

4. Where do you think you need further help and experience. Tick appropriate box.

Social Aspects: Adapting to a new ward.
Meeting people: patients
                relatives
                ward staff
                para medical staff
Talking with people
Listening to people
Answering telephone
Coping with stressful situations
(give examples)

Nursing skills: Assessing patients
Formulating care plans
Evaluating care
Aseptic technique
Giving drugs
Writing reports
Applying theory to practice
Using specific equipment
(give examples)

Others

Which of these do you think you should improve first?

Perhaps biased views lead to subjectivity where judgments are made which lean heavily in favour of the tutor's or clinical practitioner's own view. Linked with this are 'value-laden judgments' especially with such radical changes taking place in nurse education. One 'old school' nurse remarked upon a group of student nurses on a supernumerary foundation year, 'they are just like a bunch of noisy, irresponsible school-girls'. It is not easy to rid ourselves of value-laden interpretation, but it is possible to be aware of it and to design assessment tools with values and competence explicit, and with expected standards, qualities and achievements couched in positive terms.

Personality clashes are often cited as a problem; one concerned staff nurse commented, 'I have tried to get through to student nurse _____, but she doesn't like me, and to be perfectly honest, I don't like her. How can I assess her fairly?' Such honesty is to be commended but perhaps the problem could have been avoided in the first place by careful choice of mentor, stemming from discussions and liaison between ward, managerial and teaching staff.

Another problem with introducing profiling into student nurse training is the large numbers of qualified staff who are involved. In order to disseminate information to all, a constant round of meetings and discussions must be organized, together with feedback meetings relating to progress and problems. Many newly-qualified nurses and junior members of a ward team often feel inadequately prepared or trained to participate in profiling as part of continuous assessment. However, if in the clinical situation a qualfied nurse is working and talking with, teaching and observing a student during a span of duty, it is almost certainly possible to judge whether the student is confident and competent in the nursing care she is giving. The key issue in compiling a profile is whether the student is *competent,* and most enrolled or registered nurses should be able to make that judgment.

A final problem to be discussed here (there are probably more) is credibility. To what extent are profiles likely to achieve credibility in the eyes of the beholder, that is, students, tutors, nurse practitioners, managers and future employers? Profiling is in its infancy in general education and even more so in nursing education. It has therefore not been tested in a sufficient number of areas for long enough for accurate predictions to be made. Initial responses to the Dorset School of Nursing profile have been favourable, ranging from mild interest to overt enthusiasm. Credibility focuses attention upon the question of who assesses and how are they to assess? If a profile says: 'Shows initiative' how has this judgment been arrived at? A logical progression from asking: 'How was it assessed?' is: 'What opportunities have been provided for the student to display and develop this quality?'

CONCLUSION

In conclusion, there is the temptation to ask: 'So what's new?' In some cases the answer may be: 'Nothing!' Good teachers and ward sisters have always tried to motivate their students; discuss progress with them; give unbiased, constructive comments; and assess a wider range of ability and achievement than pure knowledge and practical skills. If there is a 'new' element in the concept of profiles it is that they draw together, under the umbrella of one document, all the varied elements that make students, 'whole' people, giving a much fuller picture of the Registered Nurse.

REFERENCES

Bradshaw, P. and Moore, D. (1986). 'Testing times?' *Nurse Education Today* 6, pages 204–7.

Further education curriculum review and development unit, (FEU) (1982). *Profiles*. London: DHSS leaflets.

Hitchcock, G. (1986). *Profiles and Profiling*. London: Longman.

Kehoe, D. M. and Harker, T. (1979). *Principles of Assessing Nursing Skills*. Tunbridge Wells: Pitman Medical.

Rowntree, D. (1977). *Assessing Students – How Shall We Know Them?*. London: Harper and Rowe.

INDEX